"RACE" AND CULTURE

For Ellie
with warm regards
Reene
August 2011

Other titles in the
Systemic Thinking and Practice Series:
edited by David Campbell and Ros Draper
published and distributed by Karnac

Anderson, H., & Jensen, P. *Innovations in the Reflecting Process*

Asen, E., Neil Dawson, N., & McHugh, B. *Multiple Family Therapy: The Marlborough Model and Its Wider Applications*

Baum, S., & Lynggaard, H. (Eds.) *Intellectual Disabilities: A Systemic Approach*

Bentovim, A. *Trauma-Organized Systems. Systemic Understanding of Family Violence: Physical and Sexual Abuse*

Boscolo, L., & Bertrando, P. *Systemic Therapy with Individuals*

Burck, C., & Daniel, G. *Gender and Family Therapy*

Burck, C., & Daniel, G. *Mirrors and Reflections: Processes of Systemic Supervision*

Campbell, D., Draper, R., & Huffington, C. *Second Thoughts on the Theory and Practice of the Milan Approach to Family Therapy*

Campbell, D., Draper, R., & Huffington, C. *Teaching Systemic Thinking*

Campbell, D., & Mason, B. (Eds.) *Perspectives on Supervision*

Cecchin, G., Lane, G., & Ray, W. A. *The Cybernetics of Prejudices in the Practice of Psychotherapy*

Cecchin, G., Lane, G., & Ray, W. A. *Irreverence: A Strategy for Therapists' Survival*

Dallos, R. Interacting Stories: *Narratives, Family Beliefs, and Therapy*

Draper, R., Gower, M., & Huffington, C. *Teaching Family Therapy*

Farmer, C. *Psychodrama and Systemic Therapy*

Flaskas, C., & Pocock, D. *Systems and Psychoanalysis: Contemporary Integrations in Family Therapy*

Flaskas, C., Mason, B., & Perlesz, A. *The Space Between: Experience, Context, and Process in the Therapeutic Relationship*

Flaskas, C., & Perlesz, A. (Eds.) *The Therapeutic Relationship in Systemic Therapy*

Fredman, G. *Death Talk: Conversations with Children and Families*

Fredman, G., Anderson, E., & Stott., J. *Being with Older People: A Systemic Approach*

Hildebrand, J. *Bridging the Gap: A Training Module in Personal and Professional Development*

Hoffman, L. *Exchanging Voices: A Collaborative Approach to Family Therapy*

Groen, M., & van Lawick, J. *Intimate Warfare: Regarding the Fragility of Family Relations*

Johnsen, A., Torsteinsson, V.W., & Sundet, R. *Self in Relationships: Perspectives on Family Therapy from Developmental Psychology*

Jones, E. *Working with Adult Survivors of Child Sexual Abuse*

Jones, E., & Asen, E. *Systemic Couple Therapy and Depression*

Krause, I.-B. *Culture and System in Family Therapy*

Mason, B., & Sawyerr, A. (Eds.) *Exploring the Unsaid: Creativity, Risks, and Dilemmas in Working Cross-Culturally*

Robinson, M. *Divorce as Family Transition: When Private Sorrow Becomes a Public Matter*

Seikkula, J., & Arnkil, T. E. *Dialogical Meetings in Social Networks*

Smith, G. *Systemic Approaches to Training in Child Protection*

Wilson, J. *Child-Focused Practice: A Collaborative Systemic Approach*

Wilson, J. *The Performance of Practice: Enhancing the Repertoire of Therapy with Children and Families*

Credit card orders, Tel: +44(0) 20-7431-1075; Fax: +44(0) 20 7435 9076
Email: shop@karnacbooks.com

"RACE" AND CULTURE

Tools, Techniques, and Trainings: A Manual for Professionals

Reenee Singh and
Sumita Dutta

Systemic Thinking and Practice Series:

Series Editor
Ros Draper

KARNAC

First published in 2010 by
Karnac Books Ltd
118 Finchley Road, London NW3 5HT

British Library Cataloguing in Publication Data

A C.I.P. for this book is available from the British Library

ISBN: 978 1 85575 771 4

Edited, designed and produced by The Studio Publishing Services Ltd
www.publishingservicesuk.co.uk
e-mail: studio@publishingservicesuk.co.uk

Printed in Great Britain

www.karnacbooks.com

CONTENTS

ACKNOWLEDGEMENTS

This book has been made possible because of the foresight and guidance of David Campbell, to whom we are indebted.

We would also like to thank all the contributors, from whose trainings we have learned so much and who have so generously agreed to be a part of this book.

We want to thank our families for sacrificing spending time with us so that we could write this book. We would particularly like to thank Sumita's husband, Jon, and Reenee's husband, Stephen and son, Miheer. They have been our inspiration and offered us unswerving support.

In reading this book, we hope that you will (as we did) have many thought-provoking, reflective, and challenging conversations along the way.

ABOUT THE AUTHORS

Reenee Singh (DSysPsych) is a consultant systemic psychotherapist and research specialist at the Tavistock and Portman NHS Foundation Trust. She is the co-organizing tutor of the Masters in Systemic Psychotherapy. Reenee was the Founding Director of the Centre for Cross-Cultural Studies at the Institute of Family Therapy. She is the Associate Editor of Qualitative Research for the *Journal of Family Therapy* and has written and published extensively in the areas of culture, training, and family therapy.

Sumita Dutta (MSysPsych) is a systemic psychotherapist and supervisor. She is the Chair for graduate courses in Systemic Psychotherapy at the Institute of Family Therapy. Sumita works at a London child and adolescent mental health service, and at the Tavistock and Portman NHS Trust. She has published a number of papers on training and supervision.

"Race" and Culture. Tools, Techniques, and Trainings: A Manual for Professionals is a very welcome and timely addition to the series. The recursive links between our theories, our personal experiences, and our social and cultural contexts are ever present in all our professional activities and it is a particular pleasure to see all these levels addressed so thoroughly and elegantly in this ground-breaking manual on cross-cultural training. Effective training that addresses matters of cultural diversity, the effects of inequality, racism, and forced migration is essential for the development of culturally competent and confident professionals working within a multi-cultural society, and yet many trainers feel under-equipped in delivering such trainings.

The authors are extremely well qualified to bring us this training manual, having many years' experience of pioneering cross-cultural therapy and training in a range of different contexts. They have taken a collaborative approach, so that, as well as demonstrating their own creativity as trainers, they have garnered the talents and experience of many distinguished clinicians in amassing a wealth of valuable teaching material. The training exercises are admirably clear, each being laid out according to a schema which addresses contexts within which to use it, time frames, precise instructions, and notes about the possible dilemmas that trainers might need to address. This clarity will be particularly valuable for trainers who are inexperienced in training in cultural diversity.

In addition to a wealth of suggestions for practitioners working with cultural diversity in particular contexts, including refugees and asylum seekers, kinship care, and dual heritage families, the book should be essential reading for all trainers and will encourage them to implement curricula in which awareness of cultural contexts and identities are embedded at every level.

Two features of this book particularly stand out in relation to this crucial aspiration. One is the clarity of the authors' theoretical framing of each of the areas they discuss. This means that the book, as well as being an invaluable training manual, also contains an informed and creative exposition of recent theoretical contributions. Thus, as well as providing a large number of exercises for trainers to "dip into", the book provides a coherent overview of a complex and controversial field of practice. Another important feature is the way that the authors so consistently and reflexively engage with the subjective, with questions of selfhood, emotions, and identity, and on the interaction between these and the cultural contexts within which they are embedded.

Thus, this volume fits very well within two strands of the series, the provision of practitioner-friendly guides to systemic training (Campbell and Draper), and the exploration of selfhood in cross-cultural contexts (Mason and Sawyer; Krause) Finally, and again in harmony with another strand in the series, the book addresses the organizational context and how "race" and culture can be incorporated in agency contexts with interviews with managers and useful reflections on process.

I am delighted to have this original and innovative book as part of the series.

Ros Draper
July 2010

PART ONE

Overview and generic exercises

Reenee Singh and Sumita Dutta
(with contributions from Claire Dempster
and Rory Worthington)

Introduction

Who is this book for?

"*R*ace" and Culture: Tools, Techniques, and Trainings is a practical resource for trainers who wish to work with the issues raised by racial and cultural diversity in their own agency settings. It is intended as an easy guide and a "hands-on" tool for practitioners (family therapists, clinical psychologists, social workers, GPs, nurses, health visitors, counsellors, teachers, etc.), academics, educators, and students.

The book brings together contributions from professional trainers working in multiple and diverse settings. It is aimed both at those who would like to initiate training on diversity in their agency contexts or those who wish to include the important dimensions of "race" and culture into their existing trainings.

Context and history

This book emerged directly from training developed by Reenee Singh and Sumita Dutta for professionals working with refugees in their own communities, at the Centre for Cross-Cultural Studies at the Institute of Family Therapy (2006–2009). Expanding on the training in family work skills that we developed for professionals working with refugees, we (RS and SD) were invited to talk about issues of "race" and culture for students at the Institute of Family Therapy and on other family therapy, mental health, and psychology courses. We were approached by Social Services, Health Services, Education Services and agencies in the voluntary sector, all of whom were keen to introduce training in diversity and cultural competence in their settings. The trainings that we developed were carried out at the Centre for Cross-Cultural Studies between 2003 and 2008, and are listed in Appendix I.

The ethos of our training at the Centre for Cross-Cultural Studies was to include professional trainers, especially those from refugee, minority ethnic, and migrant communities, to contribute to our training. In keeping with this, we have included the voices of our trainer colleagues in each part of this book.

We were fortunate to receive funding for the Centre from Lloyds TSB Foundation, and could, hence, afford to offer our courses for professionals working with refugees free of charge. This was consistent with one of the aims of the Centre for Cross-Cultural Studies: to improve access of minority ethnic professionals to culturally appropriate training. Our book is, thus, offered as a resource to professionals who would like to design and deliver culturally appropriate and sensitive training.

How to approach this book

The book is divided into five parts. Each part will include its own theoretical perspective, followed by a number of exercises.

In this first part, following the introduction, we will outline the main theoretical and systemic principles underlining the book. We then proceed to link the theoretical ideas with a collection of generic exercises on diversity, "race", culture, and spirituality.

In Parts Two, Three, and Four, we address specific applications for professionals working with particular client groups.

Part Two is entitled "Working with refugee and asylum seeking families". Working with refugees, asylum seekers, and migrant communities often throws up dilemmas for professionals about how to meaningfully incorporate understandings of loss, transition, adaptation, and acculturation, as well as providing practical support and assistance in the here and now. This section will provide a range of thinking and exercises looking at the multiple support systems around refugees, asylum seekers, and migrant communities, and it will consider some of the assumptions and dilemmas around "race" and culture that often emerge in the work. A section is also dedicated to looking at issues of language and interpretation, which can so often be central to this work.

Part Three is designed for those working with mixed heritage clients and intercultural couples. Until recently, there was very little thinking or research on working with mixed heritage clients and families. Intercultural/interfaith couples often present to practitioners with dilemmas regarding their cultural and faith differences, with particular reference to the impact of such differences on their parenting. There is a range of original exercises in this section, developed for couple counsellors and for all professionals who work with clients from mixed heritage backgrounds.

Part Four is entitled "Kinship care: working with children and carers". In the context of looked after children, a child's racial and cultural identity is viewed as being actively shaped with every new environment and placement the child finds himself in. In this section, we explore some of the themes of cultural transition, bereavement, and coherence when working with looked after children. In doing so, and more broadly, we consider the ways in which professionals can assist people to maintain coherent cultural identities.

In the concluding section, Part Five, we explore how managers and supervisors can use some of the ideas in the book to take thinking about "race" and culture forward in their agency contexts. We discuss the advantages and dilemmas of a number of different practices to incorporating "race" and culture in agency contexts. We draw on interviews with managers about their approaches to "race" and culture in their organizations, and we offer a few exercises to help managers and supervisors work with their teams.

Needless to say, the areas that we have addressed in this book are not exhaustive, or even indicative of all the training that we have done over the years. For example, we would have liked to include a section on working with cultural conflict in schools.

Similarly, we think this book would have benefited from a chapter on working with issues of cultural diversity in child protection. However, because of constraints of space and time, we have included only those areas that we feel that we have been able to develop most fully.

How to use this book

It is important to state at the outset that, in our training, we tend to rely far more on experiential and skills-based exercises, or the use of films and group discussions, than on didactic teaching. In fact, we seldom spend more than 30% of the total allocated time in presenting theoretical ideas, in comparison to 70% on exercises. We do believe, however, that a brief presentation of theory at the beginning of a training seminar can help to contextualize the material. Thus, in each section of the book, we will begin with a theoretical overview and then go on to offer between five and ten exercises.

The number of theoretical ideas and exercises that you choose to use in your training will obviously depend on the length and scope of the training that you are asked to provide. For example, you may be asked to provide a short training (half a day) on working with interpreters, in which case you could refer directly to the theoretical material and exercises on working with interpreters found in Part Two of this book. Similarly, somebody might invite you to do a day-long training on "Diversity and spirituality", in which case you would look for relevant exercises in Part One.

Alternatively, you may be asked to provide a more generic, modular, or short course (approximately six days) on working with "race" and culture. In that case, you could base your training on this first section, perhaps dipping into some of the other sections, depending on the kind of professionals or students you are being requested to train. With reference to specific applications, you may be seeking to design a longer course on "race" and culture for those working in a fostering agency. You may then wish to include some of the theoretical overview on "race" and culture found in Part One of the book, a few of the generic exercises found in 1(C), followed by some of the theoretical ideas and exercises found in Part Four.

What we are recommending, then, is a creative "mix and match" approach to the book, depending on the nature and length of the training that you would like to design and deliver. Appendix II comprises a list of resources, films, and websites that you may want to draw on in your training. The theoretical overview, presented in the next section, includes summary sections that may be a useful tool when presenting your theoretical ideas.

Theoretical overview

In this section, we will outline a few theoretical perspectives that we find most useful when we teach professionals about "race" and culture. Within the vast area of theory and research in intercultural practice, for the sake of brevity, we have chosen to focus on a few key areas.

1.   A systemic perspective.
2.   Diversity.
3.   Defining "race", culture, and ethnicity.
4.   Theorizing "the other"
5.   MECA (see Figure 1).
6.   Dominant discourses about the self and "the family".
7.   Cultural ideas about illness and healing.

In subsequent sections of the book, these theoretical themes may be taken up, or expanded on, or, alternatively, new theoretical ideas may be introduced.

A systemic perspective

We (Reenee and Sumita) are both systemic psychotherapists (family therapists), trained to focus on interactions and relationships *between* people in systems, rather than on the "inner world" of an individual. We find that systemic thinking, with its emphasis on the multiple contexts framing people's behaviour, lends itself to theorizing about issues of "race" and culture.

When teaching professionals from fields other than family therapy, we often begin our theoretical presentation by providing a brief historical overview of the field of systemic psychotherapy and outlining the key concepts and ideas. We base our lecture on texts such as Dallos and Draper (2000), Vetere and Dallos (2003), and

Carr (2006). In keeping with our beliefs about the importance of using exercises to illustrate theoretical ideas, our favourite exercise when introducing systemic ideas is Campbell's (2000) "Making a system". From this overview, we draw upon systems theory and a mechanical metaphor (Bertanlaffy, 1968) to illustrate the idea that people in social systems are like mechanical circuits, with each part/person in a circuit influencing and being influenced by the other. However, professionals cannot occupy a meta positon or neutral position outside of the system being worked with and this places a new scrutiny on "the self" of the professional; a self that encompasses the worker's racial and cultural background.

The implication of these ideas for training is that we spend a great deal of time thinking about what systemic therapists describe as *self reflexivity*. We believe that self reflexivity is best thought of as a series of questions that, as professionals, we are continuously engaged in asking ourselves. Drawing on systems theory, we are interested in both how we are influenced and how we are influencing each other in our working relationships. Thus, we pay attention not only to how our personal experiences have an impact on our work, but also on how, in turn, our work has an impact on us.

Part of the process of examining ourselves and our relationships is an awareness of our racial and cultural backgrounds and how this can enhance or, indeed, constrain our work with clients from similar and dissimilar groups. Many of the exercises in this book, thus, seek to expand the worker's repertoire of these types of self reflexive questions. (See, for example, the exercise on cultural genograms on p. 33.)

Another key idea that we draw upon is that of social constructionism, which is not a unitary theory, but, in the social sciences, has been influenced by disciplines like philosophy and linguistics. Social constructionism questions the universality of knowledge by highlighting the historical and cultural specificity of what we come to define as the "truth". This places an emphasis on the social processes by which knowledge is created and sustained (Burr, 1995). Social constructionists would argue that an individual's knowledge of the world is constructed within a social community through language (Gergen, 1999).

As trainers, this thinking provides us with a framework from which to critique "taken for granted" ideas about families from a cultural perspective. For example, we have long drawn upon the idea of the "family life cycle" (Carter & McGoldrick, 1989) as a time related schema in which families move through different developmental stages. One of these stages is the "leaving home" stage, and this is ascribed as a necessary transition that needs to occur during adolescence. Difficulties are thought to arise if families become stuck between stages or at points of transition. However, in many cultures, we might argue, young people are expected to remain at home until much later on in their development, and it would be inappropriate to ignore or make problematic these cultural norms without duly scrutinizing the "taken for granted" and culturally specific knowledge that underlines the ideas being applied. Indeed, family life cycle ideas originated in the USA during the 1980s under the very particular assumption of nuclear families following a normative pathway.

Another key systemic concept that we use in our training with professionals working in social services or within looked after services for children and young people is Maturana and Varela's (1987) concepts of domains. In our experience of training, professionals working with child protection concerns present as keen to explore how far racial and cultural descriptions of family life can be held accountable for understanding parenting and child rearing practices. The way in which we think about these dilemmas is to distinguish between the *domain of production* (e.g., statutory duties regarding how a person behaves) and the *domain of explanation* (e.g., exploratory conversation around why someone is behaving in a certain way) (Lang, Little, & Cronen, 1990; Maturana & Varela, 1987). The statutory and agency context within which a professional is employed undoubtedly creates constraints, duties, and responsibilities. None the less, this is not an exclusive position. The professional has to work from this domain of production while *simultaneously* engaging a client or family in a therapeutic relationship from the domain of explanation. Rather than see the domains as two distinct entities, we propose an overlapping model, or a continuum, in which it is possible to co-exist and move between the two.

This framework helps us to move from considering aspects of behaviour (such as physical chastisement) to the accompanying beliefs (often from the parents' own cultural and racial experiences of being parented). Exploring parents' own cultural and racial beliefs regarding child rearing does not mean that we let go of our statutory duty with regard to child protection. However, what it does enable is that a respectful, curious conversation can take place that acknowledges closely held cultural beliefs, without which families may find it difficult to change. Child protection remains the highest context marker (Cronen, Johnson, & Lannamann, 1982) for all conversations, but does not necessarily need to silence or subjugate other ideas and stories. Crises can present people with opportunities for change, and beliefs can be a valuable resource for us to work with.

Summary: systemic considerations

- All human systems and relationships exert mutual influence on each other.
- Self-reflexivity proposes that we pay attention to the ways in which our personal experiences and beliefs impact on our work and how also, in turn, our work impacts on us.
- Truths or taken for granted knowledge are socially constructed and knowledge is always culturally and historically specific.
- The framework of domains provides a way of being clear about the duty to regulate certain types of behaviour while also exploring the racial and cultural contexts in which people's behaviour is framed.

Diversity

Although the focus of this book and much of our training is on "race" and culture, we have included a brief section on diversity, as we are sometimes invited to train on diversity.

Diversity extends beyond considerations of "race" and culture and encompasses class, ability, gender, sexual orientation, and religion. Burnham's (1993) acronym, the Social GRRAACCEESS, includes Gender, Religion, Race, Age, (dis)ability, Culture, Class, Education, Employment, Sexuality, and Spirituality as areas of diversity. We see these different levels of diversity as interacting with, and inseparable from, each other. It is beyond the scope of this chapter to discuss each different aspects of diversity in detail.

We think of class as a complex system, interacting with culture and gender. Among professionals, class, and class differences, are sometimes even more difficult to talk about than racial and cultural differences. We try to help professionals to think about their own class background and what assumptions that they might make about their clients on the basis of these backgrounds and vice versa. We try to broaden discussions about gender to include a consideration of issues of class, culture, "race", and power, seeking to highlight the multiple and overlapping relationships of power in which people are simultaneously positioned. This includes a discussion about power (and powerlessness), and, by power, we mean both the power to act and the power to define (Singh & Clarke, 2006). In a subsequent section, we will discuss the power of dominant cultural and class-based ideas.

In our training, we address issues of religious difference and the effect of religious differences on organizations and teams. Religion and spirituality are vast areas that we will touch on in a subsequent section of this part in "Cultural ideas about illness and healing". Religious differences between couples and families will be addressed more fully in Part Three of this book. The exercises that we have included in the last section of this part of the book include exercises on religion and spirituality (Exercise 9, pp. 38–39) and the Social GRRAACCEESS (Exercises 10 and 11, pp. 39–43).

Defining "race", culture, and ethnicity

When training those who are already familiar with systemic ideas, we tend to start by defining "race", culture, and ethnicity. We ask the group how they define and distinguish between these terms. In our experience, the words "race", culture, and ethnicity are often used interchangeably, although there is still considerable debate about the meanings of these terms.

From a positivist perspective (positivists believe that our perceptions truly reflect the world as it is [Gergen, 1999]), Fernando (1991) distinguishes between

● race, which describes the biological and physical characteristics of people;

- culture, which refers to the social habits and beliefs of groups of people;
- ethnicity as a sense of belonging.

Another strand of thinking cautions that we should put the term "race" aside or in parentheses, as the idea of biological generalizations on the basis of the physical characteristics—primarily the colour of one's skin—is problematic, whereas the other two terms, that is, culture and ethnicity, are more straightforward (Gillborn, 1990). We uphold these considerations, and throughout the book we will refer to "race" in inverted commas to denote this thinking. Other theorists make a distinction between ethnicity and culture, as the former is a static and the latter a dynamic concept (Littlewood & Lipsedge, 1982). Thus, ethnicity is seen as relatively fixed whereas culture is seen as more shifting or fluid.

Brah (1996), however, argues against the definition of ethnicity as fixed, because the boundaries of ethnicity could be drawn around a number of different criteria and are dependent on fluctuating political, economic, and cultural contingencies. She questions the majority–minority dichotomy, and argues that the term "minority ethnic" is problematic in that it conflates the power of the "majority" group with a numerical referent. Gunaratnam (2003) suggests that using the word "minoritized" instead of minority ethnic captures the active process of becoming a minority. Thus, ethnic groups are not formed on the basis of a shared culture, but develop an ethnic group identity through marking their distinctiveness from other groups, and because they are perceived as different by other groups (Barth, 1973; Wallman, 1979).

Although the terms "race" and ethnicity are highly contested, we are arguing that we should include the (duly examined) categories of "race", ethnicity, and culture, in our thinking. Drawing on Derrida's idea of under "erasure", Hall (1996, cited in Gunaratnam, 2003) suggests that terms like "race" can only be used under "erasure": that is, that one has to adopt a deconstructive approach of recognizing that they cannot be used in any pure form and have yet to be replaced. The subject of "race" has been largely marginalized and ignored in the fields of family therapy, psychology, and mental health (Hardy & Laszloffy, 1994;

Henwood & Phoenix, 1996). As Gunaratnam (2003) points out, the dangers of dissolving the category of "race" is that it then becomes difficult for minoritized people to claim their experiences of racism.

With regard to the word culture, we endorse Krause and Miller's (1995) double description of culture. Here, culture is both a blueprint for behaviour, thoughts, and feelings and a changing body of ideas, which is open to and for interpretation. A dual definition incorporates the idea of the continuity of cultural themes transmitted from one generation to the next, as well as highlighting the way in which there is some choice or flexibility in how cultural ideas get taken up. For example, for me (RS), as a South Asian woman of Indian origin, there are some parts of my culture that I do not question. The way, in which I like to celebrate festivals, or bring up my children, are the parts of my culture that I take for granted. However, as a feminist woman, I do not agree with some of the patriarchal assumptions and practices from my culture and would challenge them in my own life.

As trainers, we think it essential to promote both cultural awareness and cultural sensitivity in the professionals whom we train. Hardy and Laszloffy (1995) make a distinction between cultural awareness and sensitivity. Cultural awareness involves gaining knowledge of various cultural groups and their characteristics and it is primarily a cognitive function (something we know). Cultural sensitivity is an attempt to be receptive and responsive to the thoughts and feelings associated with one's own and other people's cultural background. As such, it is primarily an affective function (something we feel).

A discussion about "race" and culture would not be complete without mentioning current research and thinking about whiteness. Until recently, discussions about "race" and ethnicity focused on the experience of black or other similarly "marked" participants. There is little attention paid to the experience of white ethnicity or identity. The danger is that this perpetuates whiteness as the *absent* norm by which other or different experiences are measured (Dempster, 2009). Taking into account whiteness in a training context would involve helping participants to unpack their white privilege (see Exercises 7 and 8 on pp. 35–36).

Summary: thinking about "race", culture, and ethnicity

- The terms "race", ethnicity, and culture are often used inter-changeably.
- "Race" and ethnicity are seen as more fixed and "culture" as more fluid.
- Ethnicities can however be multiple, shifting, and fluid.
- By including the use of the word "race", we can acknowledge our clients' experiences of racism.
- A double definition of culture (Krause & Miller, 1995) views culture as both a blueprint for behaviour, thoughts, and feelings, and as a changing body of ideas, which is open to and for interpretation.
- "Race" and culture were thought of as belonging to those from minority ethnic backgrounds, as whiteness was the absent or invisible norm.

Theorising the "Other"

For the purposes of this book (and the teaching on which it is based), we are using the concept of the "Other" to refer to the subject of representations of racialized or cultural difference. When working across culture, or with "Others", we prefer the use of the term "intercultural" to "cross-cultural". This is because "cross-cultural" has traditionally been used to refer to white therapists working with those from minoritized groups.

There are many ways in which we theorize or attempt to make sense of the "Other". The four main approaches or positions that professionals tend to adopt in understanding the "Other" are the universalist position, the essentialist position (McGoldrick, Giordano, & Pearce, 1986), the position of cultural literacy, *and* the position of cultural naïveté (Dyche & Zayas, 1995). A universalist (or etic) view would focus on the commonalities between families regardless of ethnic difference. An essentialist (or emic) approach advocates a culturally specific view, exemplified in texts such as *Ethnicity and Family Therapy* (McGoldrick, Giordano, & Pearce, 1986), which contains multiple chapters seen as characterizing important aspects of the culture of a variety of ethnic groups. While a universalist position minimizes and can sometimes ignore difference, an essentialist position makes an assumption of homogeneity between families within the same ethnic group, regardless of other variables such as social class and religion. From this position, we then have "static snapshots" or stereotyped generalizations of minoritized groups (DiNicola, 1997).

From a position of cultural literacy, one can attempt to find out more about the family's background, sometimes with the help of cultural consultants. Having some prior knowledge about their cultural background before meeting a client for the first time could be viewed as respectful. However, the possible pitfalls of seeking such cultural information are that the status of the information needs to be made explicit. The worker should attempt to find out to what extent the "culturally literate" information is based on personal experience, theoretical ideas, or research (Krause & Miller, 1995; Singh & Clarke, 2006).

Dyche and Zayas (1995) argue that the attempt of the therapist to become "culturally literate" may lead to an assumption of homogeneity or sameness within a culture and a tendency towards over-generalization and stereotyping. They suggest a position of "cultural naïveté", which assumes that individuals/families are the experts of their own cultural experiences. They advocate a "not knowing" stance of respectful curiosity, which, through the use of questions, allows professionals to arrive at an understanding of the client's cultural background in partnership with them. While a culturally naïve position is, indeed, very useful when working interculturally, the possible drawbacks of such a position is that it assumes that culture is primarily mediated through language (Bertrando, 2000; Hoffman, 1990; Krause, 1998; Minuchin, 1998; Zimmerman & Dickerson, 1994), thus minimizing the importance of rich, non-verbal actions (Maitra & Miller, 1996).

Summary: considerations of theorizing the "Other"

- the universalist position (or etic) focuses on the similarities between cultures and strives to find commonalities and threads between cultures.
- the essentialist (or emic) position focuses upon the unique aspects of individual cultures and argues for a culturally specific view of culture.   (*continued*)

- the position of cultural literacy proposes that some cultural information about families can be usefully obtained (through cultural consultants and media resources) as a way of "respectfully finding out" about a person's culture.
- the position of cultural naïveté assumes a position of "not knowing" about a person's cultural experiences but of waiting to be informed by the client.

MECA: multi-dimensional eco-systemic comparative analysis

As seen from the above discussion, understanding or theorizing the "Other" is a complex task. Each of the approaches or positions that we have reviewed thus far—namely, the universalist, the culture specific, culturally literate, and culturally naïve positions—present only partial ways of explaining and working with those from different racial and cultural backgrounds. In searching for a framework that encompasses the complexity of theorizing the "Other", we came across Falicov's (1995, 1998) MECA (Figure 1).

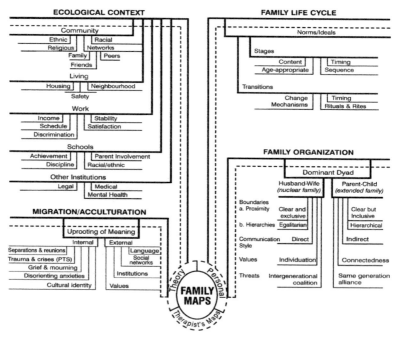

Figure 1. Failicov's multi-dimensional eco-systemic comparative analysis.

Falicov (1995, 1998) proposes a multi-dimensional comparative training framework for professionals working with clients who are different from them. A multi-dimensional approach, like the concept of multiplexity (Akamatsu, 1998) implies

> simultaneous membership and participation in a multiplicity of contexts, such as; rural, urban or suburban setting, language, age, gender, cohort, family configuration, race, ethnicity, religion, nationality, socioeconomic status, employment, education, occupation, sexual orientation, political ideology; migration and stage of acculturation. [Falicov, 1995, p. 375]

When working with a client or family that is different from one's own, it is recommended that the professional create two maps, one that depicts the client's contexts and one that depicts his/her own contexts, based on the four following key comparative parameters.

1. Ecological context: this parameter describes diversity in the way in which the family is located within its environment. It refers to the multiple contexts in which a family is located, including their work contexts, neighbourhoods, religion, and social class.

2. Migration and acculturation: this parameter explores diversity in where the family originally came from and the effects of migration on future generations of the family. The dimension of migration and acculturation reminds us to pay particular attention to stories of migration and acculturation—often from previous generations—that may form the backdrop of many of our clients' lives as well as our own lives. These stories may include an idealization or rejection of home and a process of "ambiguous loss" and mourning (Falicov, 1995).

3. Family organization: here, Falicov (1995, 1998) describes diversity in preferred forms of family forms, communication styles, and organization. Falicov (1995, 1998) points out that in some cultures, the mother–son, father–son, or even in-law pairings, may replace the couple dyad as the primary relationship. While a Eurocentric model of family development is based on the notion of the couple as the primary dyad, life cycle models in, for example, Asian contexts may be located within the

context of an extended family (Lau, 1984; Nath, Singh, & Craig, 1999).

4.   Family life cycle: this parameter describes the way in which developmental stages and transitions in the family life cycle are culturally influenced. Falicov (1995, 1998) highlights that the family life cycle is constructed differently in different cultures and that, as mentioned previously, there may not, for example, be a "leaving home" stage in many cultures. The leaving home stage, may, in fact, be as much of an economic as a cultural construction, with current rising property prices in the UK pushing up the leaving home stage to the early thirties.

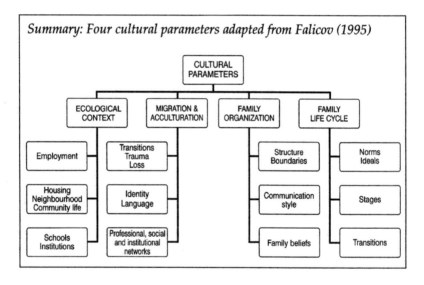

Summary: Four cultural parameters adapted from Falicov (1995)

Dominant discourses about the self and "the family"

Falicov's (1995, 1998) MECA reminds us of the importance of a social constructionist position when thinking about diversity in families. Social constructionism proposes that all truths or taken for granted knowledge are socially constructed and knowledge is always culturally and historically specific. Professionals trained to think of Western or Eurocentric models as the norm may privilege particular "truths" or discourses about selfhood and family life that may not fit with their clients' experiences of selfhood or family life.

According to Parker (1999), "the term 'discourse' is sometimes used to refer to patterns of meaning which organize the various symbolic systems human beings inhabit, and which are necessary for us to make sense to each other" (p. 3).

For example, the discourse of romantic love is a construct derived from wider social and cultural repertoires. In the French philosopher Foucault's work, knowledge is seen to be present in everyday discourse (Foucault, 1977). He argues that knowledge and power are inseparable, and, thus, depending on the power of the speaker, some discourses in our society are accorded the status of truth, or become more dominant than others. When working with clients, professionals may unwittingly impose their own assumptions and discourses about the self and "the family" on their clients.

From a cultural perspective (Krause, 1995; Marcus & Kitayama, 1991; Roland, 1991), it is generally accepted that people in different cultures think about the self in different ways. At the risk of generalizing, the Western self is viewed as autonomous and immutable whereas the Eastern self, based on a monistic worldview, is thought of as relational, interdependent, and mutable.

Harré (1986) argues that our subjective experiences of selfhood are derived from the beliefs about being a person that are implicit in our languages. In the English language, the use of the word "I" calls into existence the entity of a separate person. However, among the Innu tribe, there is no referent for self (Owusu-Bempah, 2002). Similarly, among Urdu speaking South Asian families, the word "I" ("mai" in Urdu or Hindi) is seldom used to express distress. Instead, the word heart ("dil") is often used to express feelings of anxiety, distress, or sadness (Krause, 1989; Malik, 2000).

According to Brah (1999), in Urdu speaking Asian families there are three words to indicate the different levels of closeness accorded to "others". "Ghair" is the word used to refer to outsiders. An "ajnabi", although a stranger, is a stranger who has the potential of becoming intimate, who can, often through kinship ties, become "apna" or one's own (Brah, 1999). There is, obviously, much cultural variation, with families from within the same culture choosing to draw the boundaries in very different ways.

The implications of these ideas for intercultural practice are that the ways in which we define who constitutes "family", and who lies outside the boundaries of "family" may vary considerably from one cultural grouping to another. According to Bourdieu (1988, p. 66),

> Every time we use a classificatory concept like "family", we are making both a description and a prescription, which is not perceived as such because it is (more or less) universally accepted and goes without saying. We tacitly admit that the reality to which we give the name "family" and which we place in the category of "real" families is a family in reality.

Discourses about "the family" occupy a vast area, embracing culturally specific beliefs about sexuality, reproduction, parenting, and the power relationships between age groups and between the sexes (Gittins, 1985). It also includes models of family development, constructions of childhood, and therapeutic tools for conceptualizing families. Exploring different aspects of the way in which "the family" is constructed will depend on the group of professionals that one is training. For example, when training social workers, we think with them about cultural constructions of childhood and child rearing. Similarly, when training couple counsellors, we believe that exploring cultural ideas about gender is important. As trainers, what is significant here is keeping a focus on how we can create a safe space for professionals to deconstruct and reflect upon their own assumptions about "the family".

Summary: dominant discourses about "the self" and the family

- How we define what constitutes a family is simultaneously an ideological description and a prescription.
- "Discourses" about families are culturally specific and involve the power of the speaker to privilege one description over another.
- Our beliefs about personhood are deeply influenced by the cultural lenses we apply. These views can range from autonomous to collective views of the self.

Cultural ideas about illness and healing

Most people come to see a helping professional with some preconceived ideas about what kind of help they would like, and how this help might change their lives and relationships. They usually seek help because they are stuck with a problem of one sort or another in at least one member of the family. It could be argued that the professional and the client have to arrive at a consensual definition of the problem before they can agree about what needs to be changed and how. However, it is often the case that professionals, trained in Eurocentric models of counselling or psychotherapy, and the clients that they work with, come to the helping encounter with vastly different ideas about the problem and its solutions (Acharya, 1992, Singh, 2008).

In the previous section, we explored the idea of dominant discourses, that is, those stories or sets of ideas that become accorded with the status of "truths". In the Western world, one such dominant discourse is that of the "talking cure". By the dominant discourse of the "talking cure", we are referring to the popular idea—originating in individual therapy—that feelings have to be expressed and that it is only through the process of talking that healing can take place. In the Western world, the "talking cure" dominates much of our everyday lives through the proliferation of television programmes, books, and magazines on popular psychology and healing through talking about our deeply private selves in a public domain.

Obviously, talking can mean different things to different members of a family, and to those from different cultural and class backgrounds. Instead of producing healing or generating new perspectives, talking can be viewed as shameful, irrelevant, or even dangerous. Thus, when working with clients from non-Western cultures or, indeed, different class backgrounds, it might be helpful for the professional to begin their work by "talking about talking", that is, talking about how one goes about talking (Dutta, 2006; Patel, 2003).

In many non-Western societies, talking about family matters to an "outsider" may not be considered appropriate. How do we, as professionals, then engage with families where cultural beliefs militate against talking with professionals about emotional or family difficulties? How do we position ourselves with minoritized families? Perhaps the most important part of the work is the process of engagement, to overcome the suspicion and mistrust or "healthy cultural paranoia" (Boyd-Franklin, 1989) with which white professionals or, indeed, even black professionals working in white institutions, are regarded.

In engaging minoritized families, we have found it essential to be flexible and adaptable in terms of the location of treatment. Especially at first, the work is best carried out in the community, through home visits and offering appointments in schools and in GP surgeries. The clients we work with may not be familiar with the meaning of the roles of different professionals—for example, the differences between a health visitor and a social worker—and it may be important to begin by explaining the roles of different professionals and how they are related to each other. We have found it helpful to illustrate the clients' relationship with professionals through drawing maps to illustrate their support systems and resources (see Exercise 5, p. 20).

With families whose first language is not English, or with bilingual families, engagement is best facilitated through the use of interpreters. When working with interpreters, we have to take into account the position of the interpreter in the system. The role of the interpreter—as cultural consultant, advocate, link worker, or bilingual worker—should be clarified at the outset of the work. When interpreters' roles are constructed as co-workers in the context of trusting relationships with professionals, they can potentially contribute significantly to the work (Raval & Maltby, 2005).

Instead of approaching professionals related to health, social services, or education, clients from minoritized backgrounds will often seek out traditional treatments for emotional, psychiatric, and family related problems. They may attribute symptoms in themselves or a family member to a magical spell ("Jadoo"), or the evil eye, or retribution for something that was done in a previous life (Krause, 2002). In India, traditional healers are consulted by 80% of the Indian population (Pakaslahti, 1998). Further, traditional treatments are often undertaken in conjunction with medical and psychological interventions (Nath, Singh, & Craig, 1999; Pakaslahti, 1998).

Walker (2005) highlights the fact that western models of psychological illness tend to ignore the religious and spiritual aspects of the culture that they are embedded in, whereas Eastern, African, and Native American cultures tend to integrate spirituality and religion. In the past few years, particularly since the bombings of 7/7, issues of religious difference within the UK have become of increasing concern. Jeffries (2007) argues that Britain's new cultural divide is not between different religious groups, but between those who have faith and those who do not. A recent article in the *British Medical Journal* (Sheikh & Esmail, 2007) focused on whether Muslims should have health-based services.

The clinical implications of these ideas are that in the current political climate we can no longer ignore or marginalize issues of religious difference. An enquiry into clients' religious and cultural understanding of their presenting problems could facilitate hitherto unexplored conversations about traditional healing practices and the meaning of religion in their lives. The training implications include that we, as professionals, should be prepared to scrutinize our own religious and spiritual beliefs and to explore the limits of our own tolerance towards others' spiritual and religious beliefs (see Exercise 9, p. 38).

Summary: cultural perspectives on problems and healing

- The "talking cure" discourse is a Western one that may not be relevant to minoritized clients.
- With minoritized clients, it is important to spend time at the beginning of the work in 'talking about talking.'
- Engaging minoritized clients can be facilitated through community-based work and working with interpreters.
- Enquiring about alternative explanations to problems and healing can help the professional to engage with the meaning of religion in their clients' lives.
- As professionals, we need to explore the limitations of our own tolerance towards others' spiritual and religious beliefs.

References

Acharya, S. (1992). The doctors dilemma: practising transcultural psychiatry in multicultural Britain. In: J. Kareem & R. Littlewood (Eds.), *Intercultural Therapy: Themes, Interpretations and Practice*. London: Blackwell.

Akamatsu, M. N. (1998). The talking of oppression blues: including the experience of power/powerlessness in the teaching of "cultural sensitivity". In: M. McGoldrick (Ed.), *Re-Visioning Family Therapy. Race, Culture and Gender in Clinical Practice* (pp. 129–145). London. Guilford Press.

Barth, F. (1973). Descent and marriage reconsidered. In: J. Goody (Ed.), *The Character of Kinship* (pp. 3–21). London: Cambridge University Press.

Bertanlaffy, V. L. (1968). *General Systems Theory*. New York: George Braziller.

Bertrando, P. (2000). Text and context: narrative, postmodernism and cybernetics. *Journal of Family Therapy*, 22: 83–103.

Brah, A. (1996). *Cartographies of Diaspora. Contesting Identities*. London: Routledge

Brah, A. (1999). The scent of memory: strangers, our own and others. *Feminist Review*, 61: 4–26.

Bourdieu, P. (1988). *The Family Spirit. Appendix to Rethinking the State: Genesis and Structure of the Bureaucratic Field. Practical Reason*. Cambridge: Polity Press.

Boyd-Franklin, N. (1989). Therapist's use of self and value conflicts with Black families. In: N. Boyd-Franklin (Ed.), *Black Families in Therapy: A Multi-Systems Approach* (pp. 95–121). London: Guilford Press.

Burnham, J. (1993). Systemic supervision: the evolution of reflexivity in the context of the supervisory relationship. *Human Systems*, 4: 349–381.

Burr, V. (1995). *An Introduction to Social Constructionism*. London: Routledge.

Campbell, D. (1992). Making a system. In: R. Draper, M. Gower, & C. Huffington (Eds.), *Teaching Family Therapy* (pp. 12–14). London: Karnac.

Carr, A. (2006). *Family Therapy. Concepts, Process and Practice* (2nd edn). Chichester: Wiley.

Carter, E., & McGoldrick, M. (Eds.) (1989). *The Family Life Cycle: A Framework for Family Therapy*. New York: Gardner Press.

Cronen, V. E, Johnson, K. M., & Lannaman, J. W. (1982). Paradoxes, double binds and reflexive loops: an alternate theoretical perspective. *Family Process*, 21: 91–112.

Dallos, R., & Draper, R. (2000). *An Introduction to Family Therapy. Systemic Theory and Practice*. Buckingham: Open University Press.

DiNicola, V. (1997). *A Stranger in the Family. Culture, Families and Therapy*. London: W. W. Norton.

Dempster, C. (2009). On whiteness. Personal communication.

Dyche, L., & Zayas, L. H. (1995). The value of curiosity and naiveté for the cross-cultural psychotherapist. *Family Process, 34*: 378–389.

Dutta, S. (2006). Backwards and forwards. *Therapy Today, 17*(9): 13–17.

Falicov, C. J. (1995). Training to think culturally: a multidimensional comparative framework. *Family Process, 34*: 389–399.

Falicov, C. J. (1998). *Latino Families in Therapy. A Guide to Multicultural Practice*. New York: Guilford Press.

Fernando, S. (1991). *Mental Health, Race and Culture*. London: Macmillan.

Foucault, M. (1977). *Discipline and Punish*. London: Allen Lane.

Gillborn, D. (1990). *Race, Ethnicity and Education*. London: Unwin Hyman.

Gittins, D. (1985). *The Family in Question: Changing Households and Familiar Ideologies*. London: Macmillan.

Gergen, K. (1999). *Realities and Relationships. Soundings in Social Constructionism*. Cambridge, MA: Harvard University Press.

Gunaratnam, Y. (2003). *Researching "Race" and Ethnicity. Methods, Knowledge and Power*. London: Sage.

Hall, S. (1996). Introduction: Who needs identity? In: S. Hall & P. D. Gay (Eds.), *Questions of Cultural Identity* (pp. 1–18). London: Sage.

Hardy, K. V., & Laszloffy, T. A. (1994). Deconstructing race in family therapy. *Journal of Feminist Family Therapy, 5*: 5–33.

Harré, R. (Ed.) (1986). *The Social Construction of Emotion*. Oxford: Basil Blackwell.

Henwood, K., & Phoenix, A. (1996). "Race" in psychology: teaching the subject. *Ethnic and Racial Studies, 19*(4): 840–863.

Hoffman, L. (1990). Constructing realities: an art of lenses. *Family Process, 29*: 1–12.

Jeffries, S. (2007). Faith. *Guardian*, 26 February 2007.

Krause, I. B. (1989). The sinking heart: a Punjabi communication of distress. *Social Science and Medicine, 29*: 563–575.

Krause, I. B. (1995). Personhood, culture and family therapy. *Journal of Family Therapy, 17*: 363–382.

Krause, I. B. (1998). *Therapy Across Culture*. London: Sage.

Krause, I. B. (2002). *Culture and System in Family Therapy*. London: Karnac.

Krause, I. B., & Miller, A. C. (1995). Culture and family therapy. In: S. Fernando (Ed.), *Mental Health in a Multi-ethnic Society: A Multidisciplinary Handbook* (pp. 149–171). London: Routledge.

Lau, A. (1984). Transcultural issues in family therapy. *Journal of Family Therapy, 6*: 91–113.

Lang, P., Little, M., & Cronen, V. (1990). The systemic professional. Domains of action and the question of neutrality. *Human Systems: The Journal of Systemic Consultation and Management, 1*: 39–55.

Littlewood, R., & Lipsedge, M. (1982). *Aliens and Alienists Ethnic Minorities and Psychiatry.* London: Routledge.

Maitra, B., & Miller, A. (1996). Children, families and therapists. Clinical considerations and ethnic minority cultures. In: K. N. Dwivedi & V. P. Varma (Eds.), *Meeting the Needs of Ethnic Minority Children and their Families* (pp. 108–130). London: Jessica Kingsley.

Malik, R. (2000). Culture and emotions. In: C. Squire (Ed.), *Culture in Psychology.* London: Routledge.

Marcus, H. R., & Kitayama, S. (1991). Culture and the self: implications for cognition, emotion and motivation. *Psychological Review, 98*(2): 224–253.

Maturana, H., & Varela, F. J. (1987). *The Tree of Knowledge.* Boston, MA: New Science Library.

Minuchin, S. (1998). Where is the family in narrative family therapy? *Journal of Marital and Family Therapy, 24*: 397–403.

McGoldrick, M., Giordano, J., & Pearce, J. K. (Eds) (1986). *Ethnicity and Family Therapy.* London: The Guilford Press.

Nath, R., Singh, R., & Craig, J. (1999). A life-cycle for a multi-generational Indian family. Unpublished paper presented at the International Family Therapy Association Congress. Akron, Ohio.

Owusu-Bempah, K. (2002). Culture, self and cross-ethnic therapy. In: B. Mason & A. Sawyer (Eds), *Exploring the Unsaid. Creativity, Risks and Dilemmas in Working Cross-Culturally* (pp. 19–34). London: Karnac.

Pakaslahti, A. (1998). Family-centred treatment of mental health problems at the Balaji Temple in Rajasthan. In: A. Parola & S. Tenhunen (Eds), *Changing Patterns of Family and Kinship in South Asia.* Proceedings of an International Symposium on the occasion of the 50th Anniversary of India's Independence held at the University of Helsinki, 6 May 1998. *Studia Orientalia, 84*: 129–167 (edited by the Finnish Oriental Society).

Parker, I. (1999). *Critical Textwork: An Introduction to Varieties of Discourse and Analysis.* Buckingham: Open University Press.

Patel, N. (2003). Clinical psychology: reinforcing inequalities or facilitating empowerment? *The International Journal of Human Rights, 7*(1): 16–39.

Raval, H., & Maltby, M. (2005). Not getting lost in translation: establishing a working alliance with co-workers and interpreters. In: C. Flaskas, B. Mason, & A. Perlesz (Eds.), *The Space Between. Experience, Context, and Process in the Therapeutic Relationship.* London: Karnac.

Roland, A. (1991). *In Search of Self in India and in Japan: Toward a Cross-Cultural Psychology.* Princeton, CT: Princeton University Press.

Sheikh, A., & Esmail, A. (2007). Should Muslims have faith based health services. *British Medical Journal, 334:* 74.

Singh, R., & Clarke, G. (2006). Power and parenting assessments: the intersecting levels of culture, race, class and gender. *Clinical Child Psychology and Psychiatry, 11*(1): 9–25.

Singh, R. (2008). The process of family talk across culture. Unpublished doctoral thesis. Tavistock Centre and University of East London.

Vetere, A., & Dallos, R. (2003). *Working Systemically with Families. Formulation, Intervention and Evaluation.* London: Karnac.

Walker, S. (2005). *Culturally Competent Therapy.* London: Palgrave.

Wallman, S. (1979). Introduction: the scope for ethnicity. In: S. Wallman (Ed.), *Ethnicity at Work* (pp. 2–9). London: Macmillan.

Zimmerman, J. L., & Dickerson, V. C. (1994). Using a narrative metaphor: implications for theory and clinical practice. *Family Process, 33:* 233–245.

Generic exercises

In the last section of this part of the book, we will present a range of exercises that form the basis of our trainings. These generic exercises can be used in the form in which they are presented here, or can be adapted for use in a variety of contexts for professionals working with diverse client groups. We have grouped the exercises to link with the theoretical ideas presented in the previous section and to facilitate easy access. The exercises have been clustered under the following themes:

- introductory exercises: these are "ice-breakers" that can be used on the first day, or the beginning of a training on "race" and culture;
- self reflexivity exercises: as mentioned in the previous section, these exercises are designed to facilitate the trainee's awareness

of their own family and cultural background and current contexts. This sub-section includes exercises on whiteness, to help white participants to think about their own "race" and culture;

- diversity exercises: these include exercises on the Social GRRAACCEESS (Burnham, 1993), religion, and spirituality'
- defining "race", culture, and ethnicity: a group of exercises that could clarify the multiple terms used in the field of "race" and culture;
- theorizing the "Other": what assumptions do we make about the "Other"? The exercises in this subsection include exercises on MECA, designed to link with a theoretical explanation of Falicov's (1995) training framework;
- constructions of "the family": the exercises amply demonstrate the cultural biases and assumptions that we bring to the process of constructing "the family".

The themes or clusters of exercises are intended to be mutually exclusive, and could, of course, be used in any order or combination. The exercises range in length from about twenty minutes to over two hours. We hope that presenting the exercises in this way offers you, the trainer, a range of possibilities that will enable you to tailor the thinking to your particular delivery group. We have used a standard format for each of the exercises that follow, as shown below:

- context/organization;
- aims;
- instruction;
- notes for trainers;
- acknowledgements and/or references/recommended reading.

Introductory exercises

Exercise 1: Name game

R. Singh

Context/organization

Developed at the Centre for Cross-Cultural Studies, Institute of Family Therapy.

Aim

To share the cultural and familial roots of one's name as a way of exploring differences within a group setting.

Instructions

Participants: 2+; total time: 10 mins–40 mins; resources: handouts

1. Split the group into pairs.
2. Ask them to interview each other for about five minutes each on the following questions:

    What does your name mean?

    How was it chosen? Who chose it? How was the decision made?

    What does your name mean to you, and how has it affected you in your life?
3. Agree with your partner what they are comfortable to feedback to the larger group.
4. Feed back your partner's responses to the larger group (2–4 mins each).

Notes for trainers

●   You may wish to give out sheets to each participant with the questions in point 2.
●   This exercise is a very good introductory exercise that enables people to share personal information about themselves, while simultaneously naming aspects of their racial, ethnic, and familial identity.
●   The trainers should join in by sharing information about themselves during large group feedback.

Further notes

It may be useful to give an example of how a name can affect a person. In our experience, the people who comment on this question often bring forth stories about how their name is used to mark out their difference or is felt to be a mark of their difference. It is, therefore, important to be prepared and sensitive to people naming experiences of racism or cultural discomfort. This exercise should, therefore, be carried out only once ground rules have been established.

One of my friends, Anthony Molino, a psychoanalyst in Italy, uses a similar exercise to help participants think about the socio-historical and familial determinants of their given names. Working from a Lacanian perspective, and, thus, attentive to the desire of the name-giving Other (parent), he looks at the transgenerational dynamics that help in/form the constitution

of identity. (For a compelling, and, indeed, extraordinary artistic represen-
tation of these dynamics, see the 2007 film by Mira Nair, The Namesake.)

Acknowledgement

Patel, N. (Ed.) (2000). *Clinical Psychology, "Race" and Culture: A Training
Manual*. Leicester: British Psychological Society.

Exercise 2: Speed dating game!

R. Singh

Context/organization

Developed at the Centre for Cross-Cultural Studies, Institute of Family
Therapy

Aims

- Fun and lively introductory exercise.
- To introduce the idea of similarity and difference across—not just
  with—people of "other" races and cultures.

Instructions

Participants: 6+; total time: 10 mins; resources: line up chairs in two rows
facing each other.

1. In sixty seconds, turn to your neighbour and discover three ways that
   you are similar and three ways that you are different.
2. Now switch seats, usually one row moves a seat forward, to find
   another partner and repeat step 1.

Notes for trainers

- Time keeping to be held by the trainer.
- This exercise is particularly good to warm people up after lunch time!
- You may choose to take feedback at the end of the exercise by asking
  people if they found it easier to find similarities or differences. Or you
  may wish to ask people to comment on what they found first, the similarity or the difference.
- This exercise provides a good link into teaching around different ideas
  about culture.

Acknowledgement

Thanks to Yesim Deveci, Manager, DOST.

Exercise 3: Who am I?

S. Dutta

Context/organization

Developed at the Centre for Cross-Cultural Studies, Institute of Family Therapy.

Aim

The exercise aims to highlight the systemic concept that we have multiple identities and what gets brought forward is dependent on the context and the relationship in which we are talking.

Instructions

Participants: 2 (+);   time: 10–20 mins; resources: none

1. Turn to your partner and describe how you introduce yourself in different contexts. Take 5 mins each to consider the following (10 mins):

    - at work
    - at home
    - abroad
    - to a stranger

2. Discuss any differences that emerge (10 mins).

Notes for trainers

- Give an example. For example, when I (SD) am at work, I am Sumita Dutta. When I am at home, I am Mita. When I am in India, I am Indian British. When I am in England, I am British Indian!
- Part two should be done in a large group feedback format.
- Participants often become very animated in thinking about their different names in different contexts. It is worth asking participants to consider how they would feel if their power to name different aspects of themselves was taken away from them. An example of an all-encompassing label could be "asylum seeker", "patient", etc.

Acknowledgement

Thanks to Chip Chimera, Director of Child Studies, Institute of Family Therapy.

Self-reflexivity

Exercise 4: Healing and change

Context/organization

Developed at the Centre for Cross-Cultural Studies, Institute of Family Therapy

Aim

To help participants to think about the changes that they have experienced in their own lives and their own cultural models or ideas about healing and change.

Instructions

Participants: 2+; total time: 10 mins–1hour; resources: none
   Divide into pairs.

1.   Think about a difficult time in your life or a time when you were stuck with a dilemma or problem.
2.   How did you understand what you were experiencing?
3.   What resources helped you to manage this time?
4.   What does this tell you about your beliefs about difficulties, healing, and change?

Notes for trainers

●   This exercise can bring up memories of difficult experiences and you should let the participants know that you will be available to talk, if necessary.
●   The exercise can be used on its own, or can be followed by the next exercise.

Acknowledgement

Although we think this is an original exercise, variations of it have been used by trainers in other contexts!

Exercise 5: Identifying resource and support: a mapping exercise

S. Dutta and B. Finlay-Musonda (2007)

Context/organization

●   Developed at the Centre for Cross-Cultural Studies, Institute of Family Therapy, as part of systemic training to professionals working with refugees.

- Refugee families can present with complex needs and traumatic experiences, which can make professionals working in the field vulnerable to experiencing work-related stress.

Aims

- To explore the professional and personal support systems that people draw upon to do their work.
- To enable further thinking around what other supports might be usefully employed on a personal, professional, or agency level to enable the work to be carried out.

Instructions

Participants: 2+; total time: 1 hour–1 hour 15 mins; resources: paper and pen.

Split the group into pairs. Each person should have a piece of paper and a pen. Identify one person in the pair as the interviewer.

1. (15 mins) The interviewer asks their partner to think about the significant people and support systems they draw upon to carry out their work. The interviewer guides their partner to consider their supports in four categories:

    (a) family and significant relationships;
    (b) self-care;
    (c) professional and agency support;
    (d) belief systems.

    The interviewer then maps out the responses on a piece of paper in the form of a spider diagram. Figure 2 is an illustration of what a completed map at this stage might look like.

2. (15 mins) Once the mapping is completed, and much like a genogram, the information then provides an interviewing tool through which to elicit further information on the nature and quality of relationships. For example, the initial identification of a "friend" as a supportive resource might, through questioning, yield the particular aspects of this relationship that the trainee is drawing upon, such as someone who is able to listen, just be there, or provide reassurance. Similarly, if "religious beliefs" have been identified as a resource, the interviewer may choose to ask about a time in which their partner drew upon their religious beliefs to help them manage a difficult work situation.

3. (30 mins) The pairs are asked to swap over and repeat parts 1 and 2 of the exercise, so that the interviewer is now given a chance to be interviewed.

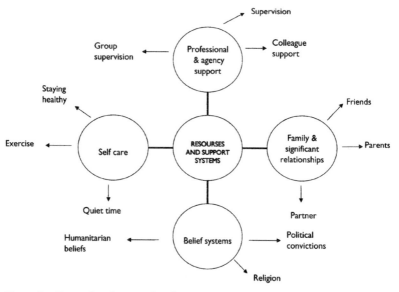

Figure 2.   Example of a completed map.

4.   (15mins) (OPTIONAL) Participants are asked to give feedback in the large group, commenting on what the process of carrying out the exercise has been like.

Notes for trainers

It may be important to re-emphasize ground rules around confidentiality, as the exercise can be very intimate. You may also want to make it clear that people do not need to share the content of their support maps in the large group if they do not feel comfortable doing so. This exercise should be used at a later stage of group training once trust has been established within the group.

Further notes

Participants are often surprised about the number of (or lack of) support systems available to them, in particular the balance between personal and professional support resources. Participants regularly feed back how empowering it is for them to name and validate their personal support systems, as this does not usually happen so explicitly.

Reference

Dutta, S., & Finlay-Musonda, B. (2007). Identifying support systems: a mapping exercise. *Journal of Family Therapy*, 29: 4.

Exercise 6: Cultural genograms/family trees

Context/organization

Hardy and Laszloffy (1995), commonly used in systemic trainings.

Aims

- To identify the groups which contribute to your cultural identity.
- To explore your own cultural experiences and the influence of these in your work.

Instructions

Participants: 2+; total time: 2–3 hours; resources: 2 × flipchart paper and pen, room space for pair work.

1. Split the group into pairs. Each person should have a piece of paper and a pen. Identify one person in the pair as the interviewer.
2. The interviewer asks their partner (25 mins):
   - for information about their families to draw a family tree of at least three generations. This can include the person's children, if desired;
   - to define their culture(s) of origin: this refers to the major groups from which you have descended;
   - to choose a colour to represent your cultural group(s). If you have more than one cultural group in your family, choose a colour to represent each group. Use both colours (half and half) to mark children resulting from a cross-cultural union;
   - to identify what aspects of your culture(s) that you believe are held to be distinctly negative or positive. Aspects to include fundamental perceptions, beliefs and behaviours.
2. With your partner, consider some of the following questions which are useful to you in opening up a broader discussion around your cultural genogram and thinking about how you use these experiences in your work (20 mins).
   - What are the migration patterns in your family?
   - What are the dominant religious groups?
   - How is social class defined?
   - How are gender roles defined?
   - What occupational roles are valued and devalued?
   - What is the relationship between age and the values of the group?
   - How is family defined in the group?
   - Have there been any intercultural marriages. How were these negotiated?

- If more than one group comprises your culture of origin, how were differences negotiated?
- What prejudices or stereotypes do others have about your culture of origin? What prejudices or stereotypes does your culture of origin have about other groups?

3. Take a 15 min break.
    1. Swap over.
    2. No large group feedback is required, and participants can keep their genograms to take away or throw them away.

Notes for trainers

This exercise should be used when a group is going to be together for a period of time. In our experience it is helpful to have this exercise, but not before Day 3. If it is a group that already has working relationships (for example, a group of RELATE counsellors), then this exercise can be used on short trainings also. If it is only a day-long training with participants who have not done much work in their own family contexts, this may not be the best exercise to use.

We would suggest, as a first step, that you model the exercise to the participants using either your own genogram or a constructed genogram. I (RS) often ask somebody to interview me re my own family of origin, or, if I do not have that person as a resource, I draw my own cultural genogram, outlining issues that are distinctly negative and positive in my own culture. I have noticed that this really helps the participants to open up about their own families.

It is important to set ground rules around confidentiality. This will include being available for participants to talk about anything uncomfortable that may arise, both within the session and afterwards. Be clear that the aim of the exercise is *not* to be nosy about each other's family background, or to uncover the "right way" to describe culture, as culture is a collection of experiences, beliefs, and perceptions. It is, however, a space to explore your own cultural experiences and the influences of these in your work.

When introducing the exercise, be clear that the first part, drawing the family genogram, is only a framework for asking the questions, as participants can often get carried away at this stage in asking for more family details. You may want to have a separate sheet explaining the rules of drawing a family tree (Appendix III).

Try to space pairs out in the room or across rooms so that conversations cannot be overheard.

Keep people on task by walking round the pairs to check that they have understood the exercise, but do not intrude upon their conversations.

Reference

Hardy, K. V., & Laszloffy, T. A. (1995). The cultural genogram; key to training culturally competent family therapists. *Journal of Marital and Family Therapy, 21*: 227–237.

Exercise 7: White privilege checklist

Context/organization

Developed by Peggy McIntyre (1988), Wellesley College Centre for Research on Women.

Aims

● To help white participants to think about their own racial and cultural background.
● To facilitate participants to "unpack their white privilege".

Instructions

Participants: 1+; total time: 15 to 30 minutes; resources: handouts, flipchart, and pens.

1. Distribute the white privilege checklist and pens to the participants (see questions below) and allow approximately 15 minutes for participants to complete it.
    ● I can arrange to be in the company of people of my race most of the time.
    ● I can go shopping alone most of the time, pretty well assured that I will not be followed or harassed.
    ● I can turn on the television or look at the front page of the paper and see people of my race widely represented.
    ● When I am told about our national heritage or about civilization, I am shown that people of my colour made it what it is.
    ● I can be sure that my children will be given curricular materials that testify to the existence of their race.
    ● I can go into a music shop and count on finding the music of my race represented, or into a supermarket and find the food that I grew up with, into a hairdresser's shop and find someone who can deal with my hair.
    ● Whether I use cheques, credit cards, or cash, I can count on my skin colour not to work against the appearance of financial responsibility.
    ● I am not made acutely aware that my shape, bearing, or body odour will be taken as a reflection on my race.

- I can worry about racism without being seen as self-interested or self-seeking.
- I can take a job or enrol in a college with an affirmative action policy without having my co-workers or peers assume that I got it because of my race.
- I can be late to a meeting without having the lateness reflect on my race.
- I can choose public accommodation without fearing that people of my race cannot get in or will be mistreated.
- I am never asked to speak for all of the people of my racial group.
- I can be pretty sure that if I ask to talk with the person in charge I will be facing a person of my race.
- If a traffic policeman pulls me over, or if the Inland Revenue audits my tax return, I can be sure I have not been singled out because of my race.
- I can easily buy posters, postcards, picture books, greeting cards, dolls, toys, and children's magazines featuring people of my race.
- I can choose blemish cover or bandages in flesh colour and have them more or less match my skin.
- I can do well in a challenging situation without being called a credit to my race.
- I can walk into a classroom and know I will not be the only member of my race.
- I can enrol in a class at college and be sure that the majority of my professors will be of my race.

2. Facilitate a group discussion about white privilege (approximately 15 minutes).

Notes for trainers

- You can devise a shorter questionnaire by including only some of the questions.
- Instead of a group discussion, you could ask the participants to break into pairs to discuss their responses to the questionnaire.

Reference

McIntyre, P. (1988). White privilege: unpacking the invisible knapsack. In: M. McGoldrick (Ed.), *Revisioning Family Therapy: Race, Culture and Gender in Clinical Practice* (pp. 147–153). New York: Guilford Press.

Exercise 8: Noticing Whiteness for Yourself

C. Dempster

Context/organization

Developed by Claire Dempster, based on her research on whiteness.

Aims

- To raise awareness and good practice among white practitioners.
- To recognize the different histories of white and black people in relation to race and racism.

Instructions

Participants: 2+; total time: one week; resources: handouts, flipchart.

1. Distribute handouts with the following questions for participants to take away and think about.

    - In what ways do you personally identify with the term "whiteness"; do you see it as a term that applies to you? What would your colleagues and friends say?
    - What do you understand might be the advantages and disadvantages of being white? What, if any, are your experiences of this?
    - Can you think of the time when you first noticed that there were racial differences? What happened, who was involved, and what do you think about this now?
    - Over the coming week, collect information about three products, for example, make-up, whose description would be explicitly or implicitly "natural", or "nude". What colours are these; do they apply to you, to your family?
    - Over the coming week, think about a social setting (not home) in which you feel both comfortable and familiar (e.g., supermarket, pub). Observe and notice what might change if you were to imagine yourself from a different racial background in this setting.
    - Often there is a discomfort in defining people as white. Nevertheless, there are activities and situations that appear to attract more white people but are not formally defined in that way. Over the coming week, identify one of these, either from your own experience or from the media (e.g., television programmes). What are your ideas or explanations for this?
    - Often, people draw on other identities to offer a different explanation of whiteness (e.g., region of the country; nationality, and religion). When do you think this is helpful and when might it not be?

3. Bring the participants back together in a group to think about their answers, the process of carrying out the exercise, and the feelings it evoked for them to do this exercise.

Notes for trainers

- It is important that any group facilitator ensures there are clear ground rules and allows sufficient time for participants to share and talk about their experiences, not least because, for some, this may be unfamiliar thinking.
- You may want to start the group discussion with a paired exercise.
- These exercises are not designed to exclude, but they do recognize the different histories of white and black people in relation to race and racism. In this context, it will be helpful to outline to participants the advantages and disadvantages of doing this work as mixed groups or not. So, for example, while a racially mixed group may prevent anxieties about exclusion, it may also risk black or dual heritage members carrying responsibility for race expertise.

Exercise 9: Exploring your spirituality

J. Avigad and R. Singh

Context/organization

Developed by Jocelyn Avigad and Reenee Singh at the Centre for Cross-Cultural Studies.

Aims

- To help participants explore their own spiritual and religious beliefs.
- To facilitate an understanding about working with clients from different religious and spiritual backgrounds.

Instructions

Participants: 2+; time: approximately an hour; resources: handouts, flipchart.

1. Break the group into pairs.
2. Ask each pair to discuss the following questions (20 minutes each): is this long enough?
   - How would you describe your religious or spiritual belief system?
   - Who are the people who have most influenced your religious and spiritual belief system?

- Identify the limits to your tolerance of religious and spiritual beliefs in others.
- How do you work with the difference in beliefs?

3. Reconvene the pairs into the larger group and facilitate a group discussion. Ask the group what the experience and process of doing the exercise was like for them and what they have learned about working with clients who come from different religious backgrounds (10–15 mins).

Notes for trainers

- This exercise can sometimes be difficult for participants who are not used to talking about their religious beliefs.
- Participants should be told to share only as much information as they feel comfortable with and to interview each other sensitively.

Recommended reading

Zuniga, X., & Sevig, T. (1994). Incorporating multiple learning goals to facilitate multicultural learning. Presentation at the 7th Annual National Conference on Race and Ethnicity in American Higher Education. Atlanta, Georgia.

Diversity

Exercise 10: Exploring social differences

R. Worthington

Context/organization

Developed for the Refugee Council training from materials used with RELATE.

Aim

To explore the range and meaning of social differences.

Instructions

Participants: 2+; total time: 30–45 minutes; resources: flipchart, handout.

1. Invite participants to think about the range of social differences as defined by Burnham (1993). This may be done by writing out the

acronym "GRRAACCEESS" on a flipchart. The acronym helps by acting as a reminder to participants. As they refer to any one of the differences, fill in the letter. You may find there are other differences (e.g., Status, or Health) that are agency specific (10 minutes).

2. Trainer continues with a discussion, that differences are always present. There are important questions to ask ourselves when we are working with others. The acronym helps remind us of the range of differences we need to be mindful about. We need to be sensitive to, and competent in, working with issues of social difference. They may be:

	Voiced	Unvoiced
Visible		
Invisible		

Invite the group to think about the differences in terms of this matrix (10 minutes)

3. In pairs, discuss for about 10 minutes the differences (from others) that are most salient for you.
    Then identify one difference which has most importance for you (there may be many, but, for the purposes of this exercise, you are allowed only one!)
    You will be invited to share this with the whole group.

	Most important to you: what do you notice in yourself?
Gender	
Race	
Religion	
Age	
(Dis)Abilities	
Culture	
Class	
Education	
Ethnicity	
Sexual orientation	
Spirituality	

4. Each pair feeds back to the larger group (2–5 mins each).
5. The trainer uses the matrix to identify any patterns, and may wish to discuss these (5–10 minutes).

Notes for trainers

You may wish to give out the handout "Social GRRAACCEESS" (Appendix IV) at the end of this session.

This exercise is one of two, which can be used as freestanding or as a precursor to the next exercise; "Working with differences". It enables participants to think in terms of the range, and their usefulness of differences.

Further notes

This exercise is more suited to being discussed by the group when the trainers consider that they have created a safe learning environment.

Recommended reading

Burnham, J. (1993). Systemic supervision: the evolution of reflexivity in the context of the supervisory relationship. *Human Systems, 4*: 349–381.

Burnham, J., Palma, D. A., & Whitehouse, L. (2008). Learning as a context for differences and differences as a context for learning. *Journal of Family Therapy, 30*: 529–542.

Cecchin, G., Lane, G., & Ray, W. A. (1994). *The Cybernetics of Prejudices in the Practice of Psychotherapy*. London: Karnac.

Mills-Powell, D., & Worthington, R. (2007). Space for GRRAACCEESS: some reflections on training for cultural competence, *Journal of Family Therapy, 29*: 364–367.

Pearce, W. B. (1994). *Interpersonal Communication: Making Social Worlds*. New York: HarperCollins.

Exercise 11: Working with differences

R. Worthington

Context/organization

Developed for the Refugee Council training from materials used with RELATE.

Aims

- To explore the way that our own understanding of differences influences the way in which we work.
- To gain skills in asking questions based on differences.

Instructions

Participants: 2+; total time: 30 mins–2 hours; resources: chairs; narrative script, eleven cards with each difference written on one side (see handout, Social GRRAACCEESS, Appendix IV), large toys or images, representing the children in the family; trainers: two (preferably).

1. The difference cards are distributed. There are benefits if this is done at random by the trainers. One (or two) card(s) is given to each participant (or pair), who then discuss what this difference means to them. How does it inform your view of the world, or what do you think about it? Each person or pair, thus, develops a statement about what that particular difference means to them (10 mins).

2. Trainers read out a narrative script concerning a family. By narrative script, I mean details about the family, perhaps including a family map or genogram. A script is provided relating to the Obama family, but trainers may wish to develop one that is more topical. Trainers (in this script) play the parts of Mr and Mrs Obama, and will also speak for the children in the family. They will then ask participants to think about one or two questions that they would like to ask this family. Trainers need to use creativity and imagination in responding to questions.

3. Participants develop one or two (professional) questions they want to ask the family from the position of their difference (10 mins). e.g., Education:

    PERSONAL POSITION: I believe that education is the way to get on in the world. I want my children to go to a good school.

    QUESTIONS TO THE FAMILY:

    To Mr Obama: How important is education to you, Mr Obama?

    To the children: How are you experiencing your dad's wish that you become well educated? What does this encourage you to do? What does it prevent you doing?

    To Mrs Obama: How does Mr Obama's view of education influence relationships in the family?

4. The family, consisting of Mr and Mrs Obama, (who will also speak on behalf the children) sit facing their "audience", that is, the participants of the course group (5 mins).

5. In turn, each participant is asked to share with the whole group:
    ● the difference on your card;
    ● what it means to you personally (share only what you feel comfortable with);

- ask the family the questions you have prepared, based on your difference (10 mins each).
6. Continue until each participant has had an opportunity to share their difference and ask their questions.
7. Group discussion (10 mins).

Notes for trainers

- This exercise builds up from "Exploring social differences", which is a necessary precursor.
- This exercise may have a powerful impact on all those participating, because it allows them to share both personal beliefs and professional skills.
- It may be helpful to ensure there is time after to discuss issues that arise.
- If the trainers can maximize the humorous aspects of their narrative, this helps the group develop in confidence.
- About 10 minutes is needed for each person. The larger the group, the more time will be needed, possibly more than two hours.
- Instead of the Obama family, you can use another narrative, possibly one more relevant to the context. If working on your own, prepare yourself to answer questions directed from the position of any family member.

Recommended reading

Burnham, J. (1993). Systemic supervision: the evolution of reflexivity in the context of the supervisory relationship, *Human Systems*, *4*: 349–381.

Burnham, J., Palma, D. A., & Whitehouse, L. (2008). Learning as a context for differences and differences as a context for learning. *Journal of Family Therapy*, *30*: 529–542.

Cecchin, G., Lane, G., & Ray, W. A. (1994). *The Cybernetics of Prejudices in the Practice of Psychotherapy*. London: Karnac.

Mills-Powell, D., & Worthington, R. (2007). Space for GRRAACCEESS: some reflections on training for cultural competence, *Journal of Family Therapy*, *29*: 364–367.

Pearce, W. B. (1994). *Interpersonal Communication: Making Social Worlds*. New York: HarperCollins.

Exercise 12: Kusum

R. Singh

Context/organization

Developed at the Centre for Cross-Cultural Studies, Institute of Family Therapy

Aim

To introduce participants to the idea that illness and healing are viewed differently in different cultures.

Instructions

Participants: 2+; total time: 10 mins–1 hour; resources: DVD/video tape of film *Kusum*, a documentary about spirit healing in India.

1. Show a clip of the film *Kusum* (or alternative depiction of an alternative healing ideology).
2. In small groups, ask each group;
    *   to identify at least two dominant ideas about illness and healing in the film.
    *   to think about how the role of the healer is constructed.
    *   to consider how this is similar, and different, to their own cultural ideas about illness and healing.

Notes for trainers

*   On a few occasions when I have shown this film, participants have brought child protection concerns into the post film discussion. They have asked whether Kusum was at risk of child abuse, and we have then talked about the resilience within Kusum's family and community, but have discussed instances when spirit healing can be used in an abusive way.
*   You may want to show a segment of the film, or even the whole film, time permitting, as it provokes many thoughts and feelings for the participants.
*   Do allow enough time for the participants to debrief after watching the film, as it is very powerful, and they may feel as if they are still in India!

Acknowledgements

The film-maker, Antti Pakaslahti, a Finnish anthropologist and psychoanalyst.

Inga-Britt Krause, who first introduced this film and Antti Pakaslahti to the Tavistock Clinic.

Defining "Race", culture, and related terms

Exercise 13: Definitions and difference

R. Singh

Context/organization

Developed at the Centre for Cross-Cultural Studies, Institute of Family Therapy.

Aims

- To bring forward people's ideas about how or if they use aspects of their ethnic experience and identity within the workplace.
- To affirm the cultural strengths and assets that people bring with them to the workplace.

Instructions

Participants: 2 (+); total time: 30 mins–40 mins; resources: flipchart and pen.

 In pairs:

1. Define your ethnicity and what the definition means to you.
2. What distinction do you draw with "race" and culture?
3. How do your ethnic and cultural backgrounds influence your ability to work with difference (that is, people from a different ethnic and cultural background)?

Notes for trainers

- The first part of this exercise is likely to bring out people's confusion between the terms "race", ethnicity, and culture, which can then be taken up in a teaching context.
- The second part of the exercise might be usefully introduced with an example in order to model to the group some of the ways we might think about how ethnic experiences affect one's ability to work with difference. For example, as a South Asian woman, I (SD) am aware of some aspects of discrimination which may make me more confident in asking people about their experiences of racism.

Acknowledgement

Rabia Malik from the Marlborough Family Service first introduced a variant of this exercise to us.

Exercise 14: A question of culture

S. Dutta.

Organization/context

Developed by Sumita Dutta at the Centre for Cross-Cultural Studies.

Aims

- To allow people to explore their cultural experiences and consider the differences between people within cultural groups as well as across time and generations.
- To highlight the idea that culture is both fixed and fluid and open to multiple possible interpretations.

Instructions

Participants: 2+; time: 20 mins; resources: handouts with questions.

1. Divide the group in pairs.
2. In pairs, take it in turns to ask each other the following three questions (10 mins).
   - What aspects of your culture would you choose to describe to a stranger in order to let them know what it means to you to be part of your cultural group/groups?
   - If another member of your family or friendship group from an older/younger generation were here, how would they describe your culture? What are the similarities and what are the differences?
   - If you were to think about how you might define your culture in thirty years from now, what conversations might you have?
3. Short group discussion (5–10 mins).

Notes to trainers

- Can be used as an introductory exercise.
- Is a useful adjunct to teaching about culture as shifting and fluid.

Exercise 15: Cultural awareness or cultural sensitivity?

S. Dutta

Organization and context

Developed by Sumita Dutta at the Centre for Cross-Cultural Studies.

Aims

- Helps participants to make a distinction between cultural awareness and sensitivity.
- Particularly useful in bringing forward peoples own experiences of being treated with cultural sensitive and awareness within the workplace.
- Brings out important considerations from people's negative experiences, which group members often choose to share.

Instructions

Participants: 3+; time: 30–40 mins; resources: handouts with questions.

1. The trainer should read out the following questions to the group and ask people to shout out their ideas and responses.
   - What are the differences between cultural awareness and cultural sensitivity?
   - Name a time in your workplace where you had to demonstrate or experienced cultural awareness to/from others?
   - Name a time in your workplace where you had to demonstrate or experienced cultural sensitivity to/from others?

Notes for trainers

- In part one, it may be useful to make further distinction between cultural awareness and sensitivity.
  - Cultural awareness: involves gaining knowledge of various cultural groups and their characteristics. Primarily a cognitive function (something we know).
  - Cultural sensitivity: experiences that challenge individuals to explore their personal cultural issues. The perceptions of and feelings towards their own cultural background. Primarily an affective function (something we feel).
- This is a simple and effective exercise, which does not require much preparation or any resources.
- The exercise can bring forward participants experiences of discrimination and racism, and needs to be facilitated carefully, perhaps with a co-trainer. It is also important to be flexible with time in order to allow for these conversations to take place.

References

Hardy, K. V., & Laszloffy, T. A. (1995). The cultural genogram; key to training culturally competent family therapists. *Journal of Marital and Family Therapy, 21*: 227–237.

Exercise 16: Being British!

R. Singh

Context/organization

Developed at the Centre for Cross-Cultural Studies, Institute of Family Therapy.

Aims

- To explore ones own constructions of identity in relation to being British.
- To break down assumptions that group members may have of another.

Instructions

Participants: 4 (+); total time: 40 min.

1. Ask participants to form a line across the room (5 mins).
2. On one large piece of paper write "Very British" and on the other write "Not British".
3. Place the two pieces of paper at opposite sides of the line and explain what you are doing.
4. Ask participants, in silence, to now reposition themselves in relation to the two statements.
5. Once everyone has settled into place, ask them to turn to their partners on either side and explain why they are there.
6. People may choose to move position (15 mins).
7. Feed back the process of the exercise as a larger group.

Notes for trainers

- This exercise is a fun and lively exercise which often brings up descriptions of culture as something we do (like taking tea bags on holidays, supporting a particular team) as well as feel. It is, therefore, a useful teaching aid to think about the differences between cultural awareness and sensitivity.
- As the trainer you may wish to model the exercise.
- When taking feedback, it is often helpful to ask whether anyone moved position and why.
- It is important for the volunteers to de-role.

Acknowledgement

Patel, N. (Ed.) (2000). Clinical Psychology, "Race" and Culture: A Training Manual. Leicester: British Psychological Society.

Theorizing the "Other"

Exercise 17: Assumptions exercise

R. Singh

Context/organization

Developed at the Centre for Cross-Cultural Studies, Institute of Family Therapy.

Aims

- To explore the personal, professional, and cultural assumptions that may be made about us in the workplace.
- To enable an exploration of how these assumptions may affect us and others in the work that we do.

Instructions

Participants: 2 (+); total time: 10 mins–1 hour; resources: none.

1. Ask for two volunteers who will not have to speak during the role play.
2. Assign ethnicities and roles, for example:
   client: Middle Eastern female
   therapist: White, English male
3. Ask the rest of the group to brainstorm possible assumptions held by the client regarding the therapist, then the therapist regarding the client, writing them on a board for the group to see.
4. In role, ask how each person (client and therapist) felt about the exercise and about comments by the rest of the group.
   Ask them to de-role.
5. Reverse roles so that the therapist is now from a minority background and the client is white. Therapist : Middle Eastern female, Client: White English.
6. Repeat steps 3 and 4.

Notes for trainers

This exercise, by the nature of it, enables people to name powerful and dominant cultural assumptions in a way that they do not have to take ownership for. While this enables the group to explore a range of assumptions, it is important to bear in mind that some of the assumptions may be offensive. Careful attention needs to be given to naming the link to racism and the impact of racism, as well as space for group members to share their experiences.

Acknowledgement

Patel, N. (Ed.) (2000). *Clinical Psychology, "Race" and Culture: A Training Manual.* Leicester: British Psychological Society.

Exercise 18: Ace High

C. Halliwell

Context/organization

Developed at the Centre for Cross-Cultural Studies, Institute of Family Therapy

Aims

- This is a quick and fun warm up-exercise that is very good at getting people to experience the ways in which status is both defined and shaped by others through a range of non-verbal communications and attitudes.
- It can be used to think about the impact of "race" and racism on status and hierarchies.

Instructions

Participants: 2 (+); total time: 10 mins–1 hour; resources: pack of playing cards.

1. From a pack of playing cards, the trainer should hand out one random playing card to each group member. Ask each group member, without looking at the card they have been given, to place the card on their foreheads for others to see.
2. Now instruct the group to form a line with Ace High at the top of the line.
3. This line must be formed in SILENCE, without any verbal communication to convey the relative ranking of the card.

Notes for trainers

Can also be used to illustrate the power of non-verbal communication!

Acknowledgements

Carol Halliwell, Kate Pelissier and John Hills, tutors on the Intermediate Family Therapy training at the Tavistock Clinic.

Exercise 19: Multiple ecological comparative analysis (MECA)

Context/organization

Developed at the Centre for Cross-Cultural Studies, Institute of Family Therapy.

Aim

An in-depth exploration of a family, looking at different cultural dimensions of experience.

Instructions

Participants: 8 (+); total time: 1 hour–1 hour 15 mins; resources: flipchart paper (×4) and pens (×4), DVD player and DVD clip.

1. Explain the ideas of Falicov's four parameters using the diagram below (15 mins).
2. Break the group into four small groups. Assign each group one of Falicov's (1995) four parameters (5 mins):
   (a) ecological context;
   (b) migration/acculturation;
   (c) family life cycle;
   (d) family organization.
3. Give out a handout of Falicov's map (Figure 3) and ask them to take a minute in silence to think about and review the dimension they have been assigned to in their groups.

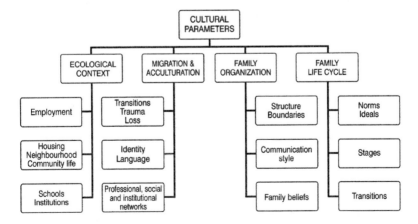

Figure 3. Falicov's map of cultural parameters.

4. Show ten minutes of a clip of your choice of film (see Appendix II for recommendations).

5. After the clip has finished ask each group to gather together and come up with one systemic hypothesis and two related circular questions that they would ask the family, if the family in the film was referred to them in their work contexts. For example, with the film "I is for India", you could say: "Imagine that the middle daughter in the family develops an Eating Disorder and is referred to your clinic." What hypotheses might you develop about what is happening in the family? What questions would you like to ask the family during the first interview? (15 minutes).

6. Hand out pieces of flip chart paper and ask each group to identify someone to ascribe the main points to feedback to the larger group (15 minutes).

7. Each group feeds back their discussion to the larger group (15–25 minutes). This could be done in the form of a "goldfish bowl" with the four presenters from each group coming into the centre, and talking about the hypotheses that the group came up with. One person in the group will present on the first parameter (ecological context) and the next person will build on the first hypothesis, connecting it to the dimension of "migration/acculturation".

8. The facilitator takes notes on a main flip chart in the room. The flip chart should be divided into four sections, one for each parameter and the hypotheses. Once each group has fed back the facilitator should ask people to look at the completed map on flip chart and comment on:
   a) What thoughts/feelings people have by looking at the completed map.
   b) What other uses they can consider for mapping in this way (such as assessment).
   c) What new ideas they have about cultural understanding (5 minutes).

Notes for trainers

This is a complex but thought provoking exercise. Introducing the dimension of hypothesizing and circular questions helps in developing systemic skills. You may or may not wish to use the gold fishbowl format for feedback, as it adds another level of complexity.

Reference

Falicov, C. J. (1995). Training to think culturally: a multidimensional comparative framework. Family Process, 34: 389–399.

Constructing "the family"

Exercise 20: Families and cultural diversity

R. Singh

Context/organization

Developed at the Centre for Cross-Cultural Studies, Institute of Family Therapy.

Aim

To explore different kinship and family arrangements across cultures.

Instructions

Participants: 4+; total time: 40 mins.

1. Break the party into three equal groups (5 mins).
2. Explain that in many Western cultures, the key dyad or pairing organizing family functioning is the spouse or the equivalent spouse relationship.
3. As a large group, ask people to very briefly brainstorm some of the advantages of this arrangement.
4. Now ask each group, taking one of the following relationships as their main focus, to think about the advantages for this relationship (20 mins).
   Group 1: mother–son.
   Group 2: brother–brother.
   Group 3: grandmother–mother.
5. Ask each group to feed back on their discussions and the process of the exercise (25 mins).

Note for trainers

You may wish to ask people within their groups to think about the advantages of their pairing from the point of view of (a) children and parenting, (b) boys, (c) girls, (d) the spouse relationship, (e) elder generations.

Acknowledgement

Patel, N. (Ed.) (2000). *Clinical Psychology, "Race" and Culture: A Training Manual.* Leicester: British Psychological Society.

Exercise 21: Family stories exercise

S. Dutta

Context/organization

Developed at the Centre for Cross-Cultural Studies, Institute of Family Therapy.

Aim

This exercise is a quick and easy way to deconstruct some of the stories that influence our own ideas about how to be a family.

Instructions

Participants: 2 (+); total time: 10 mins–30 mins; resources: none.
   In pairs (5–10 mins each).

1.   Discuss the stories in your family about what it means to "be a family"—where did these stories come from? Do some members have more impact on keeping these visions than others?
2.   How does your culture influence your family stories about how families should be?
3.   Feed back to the larger group about the process of this exercise (10 mins).

Note for trainers

This is a lively exercise that can often bring out references to books, films, or well known media families (e.g., *The Waltons* or *The Addams Family*!). A word of caution, however: it can also bring to people's mind family members who have passed away and who may have held a lead role in the family (or sense of being a family), which may be emotional for people to recall.

Acknowledgement

Nasima Hussein first introduced us to a version of this exercise.

Working with refugee and asylum seeking families

Sumita Dutta
(Contributors: Andrew Keefe, Jocelyn Avigad,
Yesim Deveci, Robin Ewart-Biggs, Karen Jacob,
and Renos Papadopoulos)

Theoretical overview

This section will consider aspects of the refugee and asylum seeking experience. It will explore the themes of identity, transition, migration, and working with issues of language and interpretation.

Who is this section for?

The section is aimed most directly at professionals working with refugees and their families. It is, however, relevant to anyone who wants to consider the impact of migration, transition, and change.

Moving beyond trauma

For some time now, there has been a tendency to define the refugee experience in terms of the trauma that has led people to take flight from their country of origin. In his exercises, Renos Papadopoulos

(Professor of Analytical Psychology at the Centre for Psycho-analytic Studies, Director of the Centre for Trauma, Asylum and Refugees) moves past the limiting discourses of trauma to bring forth fuller descriptions of the refugee experience. In his first exercise, he draws our attention to the powerful phenomena of "home" and asks us to reflect upon how these associations influence our work with refugees (Papadopoulos, 2002). In his second exercise, he asks us to consider trauma from multiple positions, including individual, familial, social, and cultural levels. His framework of the Trauma Grid (Papadopoulos, 2004, 2006, 2007) moves participants beyond negative associations of trauma and asks them to consider the neutral and positive aspects of traumatic experiences, incorporating concepts of resilience and adversity activated development (Papadopoulos, 2007). He reminds us of the fact that the root verb meaning of the original Greek word trauma is "to rub". The popular association of the refugee experience focuses on that which is "rubbed off" or lost, which, indeed, are many and numerous. However, there is a growing recognition that traumatic experiences can also enable a process of "rubbing on", or a renewed sense of priorities and meaning that enable life to be lived more fully (Papadopoulos, 2001a,b). It is with this multiple view that we approach our training of professionals working with refugees, a focus that simultaneously privileges that which is lost, that which is gained, and that which is in the process of renegotiation.

Transition, identity, and change

In the Transitions exercise, I consider how, as professionals, we can draw upon our own human experiences of transition, loss, and change as a way to remain connected to the families that we work with. Professionals often identify feeling that there is a gulf between their own life experiences and those of the people that they work with. By exploring the process of change, rather than the traumatic experiences that so often dominate, professionals are asked to consider some of the basic conditions that enable people to manage and negotiate change. This helps participants to consider the important life experiences that they bring to their working relationships, as well as the ways in which their professional roles, however small or distanced they may seem, may form part of a wider community of support.

In a further exercise, Renos Papodopolous explores the nature of identity in relation to migration and change. In this powerful and experiential exercise, he asks participants to identify aspects of their own identity that they consider important to them. He then asks participants to reflect upon which of these identities might be lost in the process of becoming a refugee. By doing so, he takes participants on an emotional journey of loss, adjustment, and renegotiation, and creates an important reflective space for participants to consider issues of refugee identity.

In a closely related exercise, Yesim Deveci (Director/Founder, DOST) asks participants to consider how one goes about preserving one's identity after an experience of forced migration. She asks participants to reflect upon what aspects of identity are internally and externally located, and what can be preserved and potentially drawn upon as a source of resilience and strength.

Exploring migration and the asylum-seeking journey

The settlement process into the host country is often assumed as the starting point for the asylum-seeking journey. What often gets missed out are people's experiences in their country of origin (pre-flight) and the journey to the host country (flight) where asylum is sought. Although these details are routinely gathered as evidence for the asylum-seeking application, they tend to focus solely on the hardships that people face.

In his exercise "The journey of the refugee family", Andy Keefe (Manager, The Refugee Council) takes us on a journey from the Middle East to the UK, following the pre-flight, flight, and post-flight phases of one particular family. This experiential exercise asks participants to consider each stage of the journey from the perspective of different family members and professionals. Step by step, participants powerfully experience the impact that such experiences can have on the family system, with a particular emphasis on changing roles and relationships. Participants are also directed to consider some of the different levels of support that may be required at each phase.

In a complementary exercise on migration, I explore the migration journey from gender and generational viewpoints. Groups of participants are asked to discuss what particular experiences and considerations might arise through the pre-flight, flight, and post-flight phases of migration. For example, groups are divided into thinking about the experiences of being a mother, a young child, or a teenager, etc. This enables participants to consider in detail the experience of migration from one particular viewpoint while also listening to large group feedback from other perspectives. When working with refugee families, there is a tendency to assume that the refugee experience is homogonous, that is, the same for everyone. This exercise seeks to highlight the complexities of experience for different family members and to enable participants to experience for themselves some of the sensitivities that need to be kept in mind when working with families who have experienced migration.

As in the previous exercises, but with an added professional and political dimension, Jocelyn Avigad and Robin-Ewart Biggs (systemic psychotherapists, The Medical Foundation for the Care of Victims of Torture, London) look in fine detail at the process of one family fleeing political violence from their country of origin. They position participants to consider not only the lived experiences of this family, but create a reflective space to explore the influence of the professional and socio-political climate of the host country. In doing so, they highlight the need for professionals to consider aspects of their own belief systems and explore how this may have an impact upon their work with refugees and survivors of political violence.

The process of communicating through and beyond language

Over the past decade, there has been a move to acknowledge the structural inequalities that people whose first language is not English face when accessing and meaningfully engaging with public services (Corsellis, 1997). The inconsistency of translation services that have been available in the public sector has coincided with a reluctance by professionals to use interpreting services, or a reliance on using family members as a substitute (Lamb & Smith, 2002).

The lack of training available to professionals to work with issues of language and interpretation has been a recognized contributing factor. Similarly, the lack of support and professional recognition for the skills that an interpreter must draw upon has led to the popular misconception that interpreting is simply an exchange of language, rather than an exchange of communication on many levels.

In her exercise, Karen Jacob (interpreter and trainer) leads participants to experience the complexities of translation for themselves as they are asked to communicate a picture through words to their partner, who must replicate what is being spoken about. Through this simple but incredibly powerful exercise, participants experience for themselves the limitations of language to communicate and the importance of picking up on the non-verbal emotional and cultural meanings. These experiences are then connected to a set of good practice guidelines, which are attached to the exercise in order for participants to consider how to best work with interpreters in the future.

Conclusion

Working with refugee and asylum seeking families asks practitioners to address issues of identity, transition, and change while bearing in mind the shifting contexts of meaning that people find themselves in. The exercises in this chapter seek to create a reflective space for practitioners to begin to explore some of these themes for themselves, thus increasing their knowledge of the refugee and asylum seeking experience while also enhancing their intervention skills.

References

Corsellis, A. (1997). Training needs of public personnel working with interpreters. In: S. E. Carr, R. Roberts, A. Dufour, & D. Steyn (Eds.), *The Critical Link: Interpreters in the Community* (pp. 77–89). Philadelphia, PA: Benjamins.

Lamb, C. F., & Smith, M. (2002). Problems that refugees face when accessing health services. *New South Wales Public Bulletin*, 13: 161–163.

Papadopoulos, R. K. (2001a). Refugees, therapists and trauma: systemic reflections. *Context: The Magazine of the Association for Family Therapy*, 54(April): 5–8. Special issue on Refugees; edited by G. Gorell Barnes & R. K. Papadopoulos.

Papadopoulos, R. K. (2001b). Refugee families: issues of systemic supervision. *Journal of Family Therapy*, 23(4): 405–422.

Papadopoulos, R. K. (2002). Refugees, home and trauma. In: R. K. Papadopoulos (Ed.), *Therapeutic Care for Refugees. No Place Like Home* (pp. 9–41). London: Karnac.

Papadopoulos, R. K. (2004). Trauma in a systemic perspective: theoretical, organisational and clinical dimensions, Paper presented at the XIV Congress of the International Family Therapy Association in Istanbul.

Papadopoulos, R. K. (2006). Refugees and psychological trauma: psychosocial perspectives. Invited contribution to Good Practice Website Project. Can be accessed at http://www.ncb.org.uk/dotpdf/open%20access%20-%20phase%201%20only/arc_1_10refandpsych.pdf.

Papadopoulos, R. K. (2007). Refugees, trauma and adversity-activated development. *European Journal of Psychotherapy and Counseling*, 9(3): 301–312.

Exercises

Exercise 1: Refugees and home

R. K. Papadopoulos

Context/organization

I have developed this exercise in the context of my work in this field in many different training contexts, but in particular at the Tavistock Clinic and at the University of Essex.

Main client group

All those who work with refugees

Rationale for developing the exercise

To illustrate the importance of the idea/image of "home" (a) for refugees, (b) for those who work with refugees, and (c) for the actual interaction between (a) and (b) in the context of their working together.

Aims

1. To grasp the powerful nature of the idea/image of home.
2. To appreciate the startling phenomenon that "home" is an overwhelmingly positive image.
3. To consider the implications this phenomenon has (a) for refugees, (b) for those who work with refugees, and (c) for the actual interaction between (a) and (b) in the context of their working together.

Duration

10–30 mins.

Typically from 10 minutes to 30 minutes, but it can last longer and it can be connected with other elements of a training in working with refugees.

It depends on (a) the number of participants, and (b) the duration of the post-exercise discussion.

Instructions

1. You ask all participants to take a pen/pencil and a sheet of paper.
2. You say to them that you will ask them to write down something that nobody else will look at; it will be completely private and confidential to themselves.
3. You say to them, "Write down five (or ten, depending on how long you wish the exercise to last) things/items that come to your mind when you think of the word "Home"; please, you must write all five (or ten); do not think much—do it as quickly as you can and then put your pen down so that I can see when you have finished."
4. When all participants have completed the exercise, then you say, "Please look at each item you wrote and tick all those that are positive."
5. Then, when everybody finishes, you ask each one in turn to say to the whole group how many items they had ticked as positive.

The power of this exercise is the element of surprise at the realization that the overwhelming majority of the items they wrote were positive; usually, it is well over 90%, regardless of the participants' culture, professional background, age, gender, etc.

6. Then you open it up for discussion. You could ask specific questions such as: how is it that we all have such a positive image of "home"? In what way does this affect (a) the refugees themselves, (b) us as refugee workers, and (c) the work we do with refugees?

This discussion can be done in a systematic way, addressing each one of these questions separately and sequentially, and it should also include open discussion following up themes that emerge from the discussion.

Note for trainers

Participants tend to find this very simple exercise most instructive and extremely apt in illustrating the powerful effect of the positive image of home.

Further notes

This exercise connects with my approach to the conceptualization and work with refugees that emphasize the importance of "home" (Papadopoulos, 2002). In short, it shows that

1. The idea/image of "home" always tends to be "idealized".
2. This is in sharp contrast with the reality of everybody's actual and real home which combines, in varying proportions, positive and negative aspects.
3. The disjuncture between the idealized idea/image of home and the reality of home has many implications for (a) the refugees themselves, (b) us as refugee workers, and (c) the work we do with refugees.
4. In short, if everybody (including refugee workers) has such an idealized image of home, refugees who have involuntarily lost their own home are likely to have an even more idealized image of home, which makes work with them extremely difficult because that unrealistic image is likely to be at the back of their minds for most of the time. Unless refugee workers are fully aware of this phenomenon and its implications, their work is likely to be adversely affected.

Exercise 2: The trauma grid

R. K. Papadopoulos

Context/organization

I have developed this exercise in the context of my work in this field in many different training contexts, but in particular at the Tavistock Clinic and at the University of Essex.

Main client group

All those who work with psychological trauma in any context but in particular with refugees.

Rationale for developing the exercise

To illustrate

1. The complexities of the conceptualization of trauma and its use in therapeutic work.

2.   Its implications for (a) clients, (b) therapists, and (c) the therapeutic interaction between (a) and (b).

Aims

There are many learning outcomes from this exercise that are closely connected with my conceptualization and therapeutic use of trauma in different settings (Papadopoulos, 2004, 2006, 2007). The following four, at least, can be identified.

1.   To introduce the importance of the variety of responses to trauma (in general and the refugee trauma in particular).
2.   To introduce the fact that not all traumatizing effects are of the same severity, but that there are least three different degrees of severity.
3.   To introduce the concept of adversity-activated development (AAD).
4.   To differentiate between resilience and adversity-activated development.

Duration

60 mins +.

Not less than sixty minutes, but it depends on (a) the number of participants, and (b) the duration of the teaching component that can be attached to this exercise.

Instructions

1.   (10 mins) To begin with, all participants need to be instructed in the theory of the trauma grid. A concise formulation of this can be found in the paper: "Refugees, trauma and adversity-activated development" (Papadopoulos, 2007). In short, it identifies three possible responses to traumatizing experiences that may co-exist simultaneously:
     (a) A person can have negative reactions, the severest form being the development of a psychiatric disorder such as post traumatic stress disorder or "distressful psychological reactions" and "ordinary human suffering".
     (b) They may continue to have certain strengths and positive characteristics and functions that existed before the trauma—this is how I define resilience.
     (c) They may also develop some positive response as a result of their exposure to adversity—this is what I term "adversity-activated development".
2.   The "trauma grid" (Papadopoulos, 2004, 2006, 2007) should be made available to participants in a pictorial form: the easiest way is to reproduce it on a whiteboard or on a flipchart in front of the group. Here it is:

The trauma grid.

Levels	Negative Injury, wound			"Neutral" Resilience	Positive AAD (adversity-activated development)
	PD (psychiatric disorder) PTSD	DPR (distressful psychological reaction)	OHS (ordinary human suffering)		
Individual Family Community Society/ culture					

3. You divide the group into pairs and ask one person to identify themselves as willing to be interviewed about their work with a traumatized client. The other person identifies themselves as the interviewer. Depending on the time available and the intended outcome, you may wish to repeat the exercise and ask each pair to swap roles.

4. (10 mins) Each interviewer should ask the interviewee to give a general description of the traumatized client; emphasizing the key characteristics of the client's "case" that have been used so far (a) by the client himself/herself, (b) by the relevant referring network, (c) by the therapist in her/his own conceptualization of the client, and (d) by both client and therapist in their therapeutic work so far. The interviewer should make elementary notes of these key characteristics and assist the interviewee to identify these key features.

5. (20 mins) Then, each pair (the interviewer and interviewee) should collaborate in attempting to find some information that fits into as many boxes of the trauma grid as possible, using not only the information outlined in Stage 4, but also any additional observations they could have on the client right now, reflecting on what was presented already (in Stage 4).

There are twenty boxes in total; for example, does the client suffer from PTSD or any other psychiatric disorder? What elements of DPR or OHS can be discerned in the client's response to the trauma? What resilient functions has the client retained from his/her pre-trauma period? What AAD characteristics can be identified in the client now, after his/her exposure to trauma? Then, the same can be done for the client's family, as much as the interviewee (therapist) can be aware of, and then they can move on to the community level and then the societal/cultural level.

It is not important that all twenty boxes are actually filled. What is important is for participants to become aware of what they seem to know and what they seem not to know, and why.

6. (5 mins) After the exercise is completed, each pair should reflect upon the process of carrying out the exercise and discuss what it enabled them to learn. They should then identify four specific points that they would like to feed back to the whole group.

7. (15 mins) Large group feedback. Each pair presents to the group their four points and the trainer opens it up for discussion.

Some of the questions that the trainer might wish to ask could include:

(a) why do we know so little about non-pathological responses to trauma?

(b) why do we not know enough about other levels apart from the individual (or family)?

(c) what are the implications of the fact/likelihood that our existing approach is so limited and does not inform us about the totality of the situation concerning our client?

Notes for trainers

• Participants tend to find this exercise quite an eye-opener: the relationship between our explicit and implicit approach to our work and the amount of information available to us.

• It can be revealing that often we make general categorizations of our clients, for example, this person "is traumatized" or that person "is resilient". These categorical assertions are fairly global and crude, and do not tap the finer differentiation of responses to trauma and the complexities of the totality of each individual. This global and not differentiated perception can be connected with the "societal discourse on trauma" and the systemic ways it interconnects with professional and institutional dynamics (e.g., Papadopoulos, 2000, 2001a,b, 2002).

• This exercise works better if it is part of a more detailed training, specifically about the trauma grid, that examines all its theoretical and practical dimensions. However, it can also be beneficial if it is introduced on its own, to illustrate the basic rationale of the trauma grid and to assist professionals to work in a more differentiated way with traumatized clients.

Exercise 3: Managing change

S. Dutta

Context/organization

Developed at the Centre for Cross-Cultural Studies, Institute of Family Therapy

Aims

● To explore the different ways in which people manage change, with an emphasis on identifying associated feelings, resources, and resilience factors.

● To connect refugee workers to their own experiences of managing change and how these experiences can be used as a resource in their work with refugee families.

Instructions

Participants: 4+; duration: 1 hour; resources: 3 × flipcharts and pens

1. Break the group into pairs and spread out across the room.
2. Ask each pair to identify themselves as an interviewer and an interviewee.
3. Ask the interviewee to think about one big *planned* change that they are willing and comfortable to share. Ask them to take a few minutes to consider and remember this change (5 mins).

    Now ask the interviewer to interview their partner about this change, asking questions around the following areas (10 mins).

    (a) What can you remember feeling around that time?

    (b) In what ways were you able to prepare or rehearse for the change?

    (c) What people, resources, and other experiences where you able to draw upon?

4. Now ask the interviewee to think about a change that they were *not able to plan*. Ask them to take a few minutes to consider and remember this change.

    Now ask the interviewer to interview their partner about this change, asking the same questions around the following areas (10 mins).

    (a) What can you remember feeling around that time?

    (b) In what ways were you able to prepare or rehearse for the change?

    (c) What people, resources, and other experiences where you able to draw upon?

5. Swap roles in each partnership so that the interviewer now has a chance to be interviewed. Repeat stages 3 and 4 (20 mins).
6. Bring the group back together and ask participants to feed back to the larger group their experience of carrying out this exercise. This does not need to include details of their conversations, but should focus on their main learning points and links to their work with refugees (15–30 mins).

Notes for trainers

● This exercise touches on peoples own experiences of loss, transition, and change and can evoke powerful emotions connected to resilience and the need for resources.
● Participants usually want to spend some time processing these emotions, and find it useful to think about how these experiences link to their work with refugees.
● It is interesting to note that many participants find it easier to think about an unplanned change than a planned one. This touches upon the popular view that change is usually accompanied by a loss of control.

Exercise 4: Refugee identity

R. K. Papadopoulos

Context/organization

I have developed this exercise in the context of my work in this field in many different training situations, but in particular at the Tavistock Clinic and at the University of Essex.

Main client group

All those who work with refugees.

Rationale for developing the exercise

To illustrate the importance of the (a) refugee identity, (b) the different ways one can understand the changes that occur when one becomes a refugee, and (c) the difficulties that language creates in communicating with refugees.

Aims

1. To grasp the powerful nature of the refugee identity.
2. To appreciate the startling phenomenon and different meanings the word "change" may have.

3.   To consider the implications this phenomenon has (a) for refugees, (b) for those who work with refugees, and (c) for professional interactions between refugees and the professionals who work with them.

Duration

10–30 mins.

Typically from ten minutes to thirty minutes, but it can last longer and it can be connected with other elements of a training in working with refugees.

It depends on (a) the number of participants, and (b) the duration of the post exercise discussion.

Instructions

1.   You ask all participants to take a pen/pencil and a sheet of paper.
2.   You say to them that you will ask them to write down something that nobody else will look at; it will be completely private and confidential to themselves.
3.   You say to them, "Write down ten things/items that answer the question: "Who am I?" Write down whatever you think characterizes you, whatever comes to your mind. It is important that you write all ten items. Write as quickly as you can, and then put your pen down so that I can see when you finish."
4.   When all participants have completed the exercise, you say,
     "Imagine you have now become a refugee. Please read carefully each one of the ten things/items you wrote and tick all those that you think are likely to change as a result of you becoming a refugee. Then, please count how many items you have ticked."
5.   Then, when everybody finishes, you ask each one in turn to say to the whole group how many items they have ticked.
     It is very likely that this exercise will produce a very wide variation of how many items were ticked.
6.   Then you open it up for discussion.
     ● When one becomes a refugee, what do you think changes and what do you think does not change?
     ● Why is there such a wide variation of responses?
     ● What makes us understand this simple question in so many different ways?
     ● What are the implications of this phenomenon (a) for the refugees themselves, (b) for us as refugee workers, and (c) for the work we do with refugees?

This discussion can be done in a systematic way, addressing each one of these questions separately and sequentially, and it should also include open discussion, following up themes that emerge from the discussion.

Note for trainers

The power of this exercise is the element of surprise at the realization that the simple instruction of attempting to identify what changes when one becomes a refugee is not so simple, after all, and it opens up many questions: for example, what changes and what does not change and what do we mean by change; change as defined or experienced by whom?

Further notes

Most probably, participants will say that what does not change are what could be called "essential" characteristics of a person, for example, the fact that they are a man or a woman, that they are a wife or a son, the fact that they are social workers or psychologists, etc. However, the picture is much more complex. If this does not come up in the discussion, I bring up my own experiences of hearing refugees say "After what happened to me, I will never be a woman (or a mother, or a father) again". This refers to their subjective experience of what they understand by those "essential" identity markers, such as "woman", "man", "husband", "mother", etc. In other words, this exercise shows that in addition to the objective, demographical elements/dimensions/markers of identity (i.e., what is written in the refugees' passports or other official documents), each person construes these "essential" elements in a unique way that is affected by their own personal experiences; the unique meaning that refugees attach to aspects of their identity is not usually accessible to others, and they may not be fully aware of it themselves, either.

Usually, we think that when people become refugees, only certainly aspects of their lives change, for example, their living conditions, their social or financial status, etc., whereas other characteristics that are considered to be "essential" do not change (e.g., gender, age, family status). Yet, this is not the case, and this exercise brings up the complexity not only of what changes and what does not change, but also what constitutes change and who defines change.

This exercise connects with my approach to the conceptualisation and work with refugees that emphasise the importance of the role of the 'mosaic substratum of identity' and 'nostalgic disorientation' in the formation of the refugee identity (Papadopoulos, 1997, 2001a,b, 2002)

Exercise 6: Exploring the impact of forced migration on identity

Y. Deveci

Context/organization

Developed by Dost, Trinity Centre.

Aims

- To enable participants to explore the aspects of their identity which are most important to them and to reflect upon how these might be affected by the process of forced migration.
- To consider which aspects of self can be preserved in exile.

Instructions

Participants: 6–10; total time: 1 hour; resources: A4 paper and pens.

(A) Part one: Identity (10 mins)

1. Give each participant a piece of A4 paper and a pen and ask them to divide the sheet of paper into eight equal boxes.
2. Explain that the next part of the activity can be done in private and does not need to be shared.
3. Ask participants to write in each box an aspect of their identity that is most important to them (that is, eight aspects of their identity in total).

Part two: Loss (20 mins)

1. When everyone has finished, explain that they have to lose one aspect of their identity. Ask the participants to put a line through the word/s they have chosen.
2. Repeat this activity until there are no more words left. This exercise becomes increasingly difficult as fewer and fewer words remain.
3. Ask the participants for feedback on the experience of participating in the exercise.
4. If appropriate, the trainer can ask the participants to think about the aspects of their identities which are most important to them and which of these aspects may be lost or affected by forced migration.

(B) Part three: Preserving self (30 mins)

1. Divide the group into pairs.
2. (10 mins) Ask each pair to choose one aspect of their own identity and discuss how this might be preserved in exile.
3. (10 mins) Ask each pair to take it in turns to feed back their ideas to the large group.
4. (10 mins) The trainer should then encourage the whole group to think about the impact of forced migration on identity, and ways of preserving aspects of one's identity in exile.

Notes for trainers

- This exercise is intended to help participants begin to connect with the experience of forced migration. The emphasis is, therefore, on enabling participants to think about their own sense of identity: which aspects are internal, which are external, which aspects might be lost in a process of forced migration, and what can be preserved and potentially drawn on as a source of strength?

- This is a very personal exercise and individual interpretations and responses vary greatly. It is important for the trainer to allow enough time for personal reflection. Where appropriate, the trainer may emphasize the subjective nature of the exercise and encourage participants to think about their own experiences.

Acknowledgement

This exercise has been adapted from a presentation given by John Flynn, family therapist and nurse specialist, Ealing Child & Adolescent Mental Health Team.

Recommended reading

Papadopoulos, R. 1997, 2001a,b, 2002.

Exercise 7: The journey of the refugee family

A. Keefee

Context/organization

The Refugee Council Specialist Support Service in Brixton, South London. The exercise concerns the experience of a fictional family fleeing from a "Middle Eastern country". The events described are based on actual experiences of clients as related to us through our work. The workshop is delivered as part of a course introducing a range of systemic theory and skills, applied in particular to refugee families.

Aims

- To explore some of the experiences and journeys of refugee families travelling to the UK, including the pre-flight, flight, and post-flight phases.
- To gain awareness of the impact such experiences can have on the family system, roles, and relationships.
- To consider different levels of support required at each phase.

Instructions

Participants: 12–25; total time: 2–3 hours.

1. Introduction to the group: divide the group into four, and seat them in different areas of the room.

2. Explain that the exercise will follow the experience of a family fleeing from their home in a Middle Eastern country to join relatives in the UK. The family is forced to leave their home when the father is arrested at an anti-government demonstration and tortured.

3. Ask one group to volunteer to role-play the travelling family. This should ideally be a group of four. You should stress that this is not a role play in the sense that participants will not be required to *act*. Rather, each will be asked to hold their role in mind and think about the events described from the perspective of the person they represent.

4. Now assign the other three groups to take on
    (a) roles as the extended family in the Middle Eastern country of origin (4–8);
    (b) the relatives in London (4);
    (c) a group of professionals in the UK (4–6).
    As before, each group are asked to hold in mind how they might be feeling at different stages of the journey.

5. Now assign roles within each group and ask people to choose roles within their groups. First, you are going to introduce the family. The "travelling" family consists of Ali (36), his wife Fatima (32), their son, Hassan (12), and daughter, Mariam, 8. Ali and Fatima have extended family on both sides (parents, brothers and sisters, aunts, uncles, and cousins) that remain behind in their country of origin. The travelling family journey to London to stay with Ali's older brother, Kemal (40), his wife, Nazreen, and their children, Khashif (13), and Nousheen (9).

6. Now arrange seating so that there are distinct groups, the travelling family, Ali's family at home, Fatima's family at home, the receiving family in the UK, and professionals in the UK.

7. At this point you will tell the group that you are going to read the story of the family's journey. Inform the group that you will pause at key moments in the journey and ask different group members how they feel about what is happening from their various perspectives. Some sample questions are included in the text. Remember to ask participants how they think *other* people might be feeling, as well as how they may actually be feeling themselves.

Ali is a teacher who becomes involved in trade union activities and starts to go on demonstrations protesting against repressive labour practices. He is detained and tortured and is very traumatized and frightened afterwards. He decides to leave and take his family with him. Ali borrows money from his father and in-laws and pays an agent to take them to London.

Pause, question (to travelling family)

How do Ali's children feel when they are told they are leaving? What information is shared and among whom? What planning/packing needs to be done and by whom? How do Ali's and Fatima's parents/extended family feel? How is Ali's brother's family in London informed? What are the responses of each family member?

The journey begins with a walk over the mountains at night and takes three months. Much of the time is spent hiding from the authorities in the countries they pass through. They travel in the backs of lorries without sanitary facilities or much to eat or drink. They spend days at a time in lorries, often with strangers, and have to use plastic bags for toilets. They often have to sleep outside.

Pause, question:
What is it like being on the journey? What is it like waiting for news of the travelling family?

Ali and his family don't know where they are most of the time and are constantly frightened. They have to cross a lake on an overcrowded boat: the smugglers throw two people off the boat and they drown. Someone else they meet falls off a lorry and is killed.

The family eventually reaches London and move in with Kemal. Ali has not seen Kemal for ten years since he left to claim asylum in the UK. Kemal has full refugee status and lives in a two-bedroom flat in North London. There are now four adults and four children living in the flat.

Pause, question:
Where is everyone going to sleep? What is it like discussing this? Will there be conflicts about when to go to bed if someone has to sleep in the living room?

How do the cousins get along? How does Khashif feel about introducing Hassan to his friends? How does Mariam feel about Nousheen? How does Nousheen feel about sharing her toys with Mariam?

How does Ali get on with Kemal? How has their relationship changed in the ten years Kemal has been away?

How do the sisters-in-law feel about each other? What is it like for Fatima to live in the house of her husband's older brother?

After a few weeks, Ali starts sleeping badly: he wakes up screaming several times a night and often gets up to have a cigarette in the kitchen. Sometimes he goes into the front room and turns the television on.

Pause, question:
How do the other people in the flat react to this? Why do they think Ali is behaving like this? How does Ali feel about it?

News arrives from home: Fatima's brother has been arrested by police looking for Ali. He has been in custody for four days and the family are worried he is being tortured.

Pause, question

How do Ali and Fatima feel about this? How do Fatima's relatives now feel about Ali? How do Hassan and Mariam think the news is affecting their parents?

Ali wants to move his family into a flat of his own. He takes advice from a refugee agency, but is told the family would have to move to Glasgow. He and Fatima are worried about being away from people they know, so they decide to stay.

Pause, question:

How does everyone feel about the idea of Ali and Fatima wanting to move out? What about them deciding to stay? How does Ali imagine his sister-in-law feels?

Finally, a year later, the family is still living in the flat and has not been granted status yet. Ali's son is getting into fights at school and playing truant. He discloses to his teacher that he has started cutting himself and the family is referred to a family therapy service. The last section of the exercise is therefore a consultation with the Team:

Pause, question:

The professional team should be asked to discuss what they think is going on in the family. Family members may be asked how they feel, or think about the brother's difficulties.

1. End of exercise: It is very important to de-role: ask participants to return to their original seat in the room, and then stand up one by one to say "I am not (my character in the exercise), I am (real name) and after the training I will . . ."
2. Once everyone has de-roled, ask participants to comment on the process and experience of carrying out the exercise. Ask people what personal connections they have made, what professional connections they have made, what new learning they have gained about the refugee experience and how they might incorporate this into their work?

Notes for trainers

For systemic practitioners, you may like to use a genogram to encourage participants to think about the dynamics within the family and points of transition, for instance.

For other professionals, a family tree, showing the names, ages, and relationships of the family members and extended family may make the exercise clearer for participants.

A floor plan showing the layout of the flat in London can also help: there should be a hallway with two bedrooms, a bathroom, kitchen, and living room.

De-roleing at the end of the exercise is very important.

Feedback from participants has always included how powerful and complex this exercise is in helping them to consider the many layers of the refugee experience and transitions.

Exercise 8: Exploring migration

S. Dutta

Context/organization

Developed at the Centre for Cross-Cultural Studies, Institute of Family Therapy.

Aims

- To explore the different ways in which family members experience the process of migration and post settlement, depending on gender and age.
- To consider in detail some of the ways in which people journey to the UK and experience post settlement.

Instructions

Participants: 6 (+); total time: 1 hour; resources: 3× flipchart and pens.

1. Break the group into three separate groups and ask them to spread out across the room. Give each group a piece of flipchart paper and pen. Ask one member of each group to take responsibility for transcribing the main points from the discussion on to the flipchart and feeding back to the large group at the end.
2. Give each group one of the following three categories:
    - men;
    - women;
    - children.
3. (20 mins) Now let the group know that you want them to brainstorm, from the position of their assigned roles, what experiences this population may have of
    (i) the migration journey,

(ii)   post settlement experiences.
4.   (30 mins) Ask each group to take it in turns to feed back their ideas to the large group. This should take about ten minutes per group.
5.   (10 mins) The trainer should then encourage the whole group to think about the total experiences identified so far, including some of the associated emotions that arise.

Notes for trainers

● This exercise is a highly participatory and fruitful way for students to think about the fine details of how people experience migration and post settlement in a new country.

● Most groups identify some of the difficult experiences that people can face in refugee camps and some of the financial, language, and employment barriers they face in the new country. If they do not, it is useful for the trainer to prompt them to think about these areas. This can be done by the trainer walking round each group during the brain-storming section to check that people are on track.

● Given the nature of the exercise, it is likely to touch on people's painful and possibly racist or abusive experiences of coming to and settling in a new country. It is, therefore, important to leave at least ten minutes at the end of the exercise to help trainees process any associated emotions or issues that might arise.

Acknowledgement

This exercise is based on a lecture given by Amal Treacher, Associate Professor, School of Sociology and Social Policy, Nottingham University.

Exercise 9: Family reunion

J. Avigad and R. Ewart-Biggs

Context/organization

Jocelyn Avigad and Robin Ewart-Biggs (Medical Foundation for the Care of Victims of Torture) created this exercise for workshops on working with families who have suffered torture/organized violence.

Aims

● To consider different layers of context in relation to work with refugee families.

● To consider cultural meeting points between refugee families and professionals.

- To raise awareness about the dominant stories and themes concerning refugee families in the 'host country'.

Duration

50–60 mins.

Number of participants

12–40

Instructions

1. (5mins) Break the large group into four sub-groups and ask each group to sit in a circle, spreading the four groups out across the room. Explain that you are going to present a case example and that you want each sub-group to approach the case using a different lens:
   - Group A—individual family members;
   - Group B—family as a whole;
   - Group C—professionals;
   - Group D—socio-political context.
2. (10 mins) The trainer should ask group members whether they would like to present a case example from their own work with a refugee family, giving details of referral information and family presentation. Alternatively, you may use the example below:

Family A has been referred to your service by their GP, with the following information: Mr A has been in the UK for two years, having left his own country, where he had been a member of a banned political party and detained as a result. Having been granted leave to remain in the UK, he has recently been joined by his wife and two of their children, aged fifteen and eight. They had themselves been displaced during the past year due to civil war, during which time they became separated from their two older children, whose whereabouts are not known. There are strong suggestions that Mr A and possibly other family members have been tortured and ill-treated. The GP is treating both parents for depression and also anxiety symptoms with the father. The GP is concerned about the deteriorating family relationships/communication and there are also concerns about the children's difficulty in engaging at school.

3. (32 mins) The trainer now asks each group in turn (A–D) to hold a "reflecting conversation" where they discuss the case material from their allocated perspective. This is a spontaneous conversation where ideas and thoughts are shared and developed. Groups do not need time to prepare.

(a) Each group should sit in a circle facing each other and talking among themselves as the other groups listen (approximately eight minutes per group).

(b) Group members should be encouraged to
   - talk about their initial responses to the family information from their allocated perspective (of individual family members/ family as a whole/professional/ socio-political);
   - think about what professional considerations they might have in starting to work with this family.

4. (5–15mins) After each group has discussed their thoughts, ask everyone to reposition their chairs into a large group format and discuss with the group their experience of carrying out this exercise, both in terms of process and content.

Notes for trainers

- Ask the groups to bear in mind issues of difference that might arise in relation to both the family and the professional's cultures, for example, ethnicity, nationality, religion, etc.
  Also encourage people to remember that some family members have Leave to Remain (legal status conferring rights to stay in UK following successful asylum application) while others do not.
- If group members are not familiar with "reflecting conversations", they may need help to keep focused on the groups' particular lens and participants usually need some prompting to talk only with other sub group members rather than to the large group itself.
- The exercise has the potential to generate many different ideas and reactions, which are likely to reflect the number of perspectives relevant to working with refugee families.

Exercise 10: How do we communicate?

K. Jacob

Context/organization

I first started to use this exercise when delivering training in early years' care and education. Over the past six years, I have adapted the exercise for trainings aimed at practitioners who use interpreters.

Aims

- To explore the limitations of language in communication.
- To consider the important role of non-verbal cues in communication.
- To question our assumptions about shared meanings.
- To consider how we can make effective use of interpreters in our work.

Instructions

Participants: 2 (+) pairs; total time: 50 mins–1 hour; resources: two sheets of paper and pen per participant.

1. Each pair should place their chairs so that they are sitting back to back.
2. Each participant should have with them a sheet of paper and a pen.
3. Ask one participant to draw a fairly simple drawing (e.g., a house, cat, geometric shape) (5 mins).
4. Once the drawing is complete, the participant who did the drawing should attempt to describe to their partner exactly what they have drawn in order for the other person to attempt to copy the picture described. They can use any words, but cannot turn around to look at each other or the drawing (10 mins).
5. Partners should switch roles and repeat points 2–4 (15 mins).
6. Once finished, pairs should compare drawings (5 mins).
7. Large group feedback on the process of carrying out the exercise (15–25 mins).

Notes for trainers

- It is important to stress that the objective of the exercise is to make a copy of the drawing made by your partner that is as accurate as possible.
- Please stress to participants that in describing the drawing they may use any verbal cues but at no time should they make eye contact with each other, use gestures, or see each other's drawings until the exercise is completed.
- This is a really fun and lively exercise, but it can also stir up frustrations.
- Questions that regularly arise during large group feedback include:
    - How accurate were the copies?
    - How difficult was it to describe one's drawing?
    - How difficult was it to understand your partner's description? Did you have to seek clarification? Did you misunderstand any instructions?
    - How hard was it not seeing your partner? How hard was it not using gestures?
    - Did you make any cultural/knowledge assumptions. For example, a participant assumed that their partner would know what Mickey Mouse would look like. Another participant assumed that their partner would use inches rather than centimetres to judge length.
    - Did anyone inadvertently compete, or did everyone co-operate fully with their partner? Participants can sometimes unconsciously

withhold information (such as naming the object) without realizing it.
- Encourage participants to make links between their learning from the exercise and how this makes them think about the effective use of interpreters in their work.
- Finish by considering the following guidance on working with interpreters.

Working with an interpreter: good practice guidance

Practical things

1. Check the interpreter and the client speak the same language and dialect.
2. Allow time for pre-interview discussion with the interpreter to talk about the objectives of the interview and the way in which you will work together.
3. Ask the interpreter how to pronounce the client's name correctly.
4. Always speak directly to the client and actively listen to what the interpreter and client are saying.
5. Allow time
   - for the interpreter to introduce himself/herself to the client and explain his/her role;
   - to explain that the interview will be confidential;
   - to check whether the interpreter is acceptable to the client;
   - to introduce yourself and your role to the client.
5. Encourage the interpreter to interrupt and intervene during the consultation if necessary.
6. Use straightforward language and avoid jargon.
7. Allow enough time for consultation (perhaps twice as long as for an English speaking client).
8. At the end of the interview, check that the client has understood everything or whether he/she wants to ask anything else.
9. Have a post-interview discussion with the interpreter.

Things to remember.

1. The pressure is on the interpreter.
2. As the clinician, the responsibility for the interview is yours.
3. Your power as a clinician, as perceived by the interpreter and the client.
4. To show patience and compassion in a demanding situation.
5. To be aware of your own attitudes towards those who are different from you, including awareness of racism.

6. To show respect for the interpreter and his/her skills.

Points to check if things seem to be going wrong in the interview.

1. Does the interpreter speak English and the client's language fluently?
2. Is the interpreter acceptable to the client (for example, gender, age, religion)?
3. Is the client prevented from telling you things because of his/her relationship to the interpreter?
4. Are you creating as good a relationship as possible with your client?
5. Is the interpreter translating what you and your client are saying or is he/she advancing his/her own views and opinions?
6. Does the interpreter understand the purpose of the interview and his/her role?
7. Have you given the interpreter time to meet the client and explain his/her role?
8. Does the interpreter feel free to interrupt you if necessary to indicate problems or seek clarification?
9. Are you using simple jargon-free English?
10. Is the interpreter ashamed or embarrassed by the client or the subject of the consultation?
11. Are you allowing the interpreter enough time?
12. Are you maintaining as good a relationship as you can with the interpreter (for example, by showing respect for his/her skills and maintaining an awareness that the interpreter is probably under pressure)?

Acknowledgement

Loosely based on *The Right to be Understood* by Jane Shackman (1984) (National Extension College).

PART THREE

Working with mixed heritage clients and intercultural couples

This part of the book comprises two sections. In the first section, Yvonne Ayo and Melanie Gabbi highlight the issues for training professionals working with clients of mixed heritage. Reenee Singh and Sumita Dutta focus on the issues particular to working with intercultural and interfaith couples in the second section.

A. Working with clients of mixed heritages

Yvonne Ayo and Melanie Gabbi

Introduction

When people who don't know me well, black or white, discover my background (and it is usually a discovery, for I ceased to advertise my mother's race at the age of twelve or thirteen, when I began to suspect that by doing so I was ingratiating myself to whites), I see the split-second adjustments they have to make, the searching of my eyes for some telltale sign. They no longer know who I am. Privately, they guess at my troubled heart, I suppose—the mixed blood, the divided soul, the ghostly image of the tragic mulatto trapped between two worlds. [Obama, 2007]

Obama achieved the dream of becoming the first black president of the USA in January 2009 and his experience of being mixed race— the searching look, the uncertainty of people he meets not knowing who he really is, and their private thoughts of how they may really perceive him—forms part of the general experiences of many mixed race persons. It is an identity that is sometimes characterized as marginal, detached, and confused, an identity that often assumes that individuals wander the world in search of acceptance and belonging.

Who are we?

Our rationale is to challenge the idea of mixed race identity as problematic, which attracted us to write this chapter based on our personal experiences as people of mixed heritages and from our professional contexts. One of us (Yvonne) is a systemic psychotherapist working in a multi-disciplinary team in a child and adolescent mental health service and based in two schools in London. Mel is a counsellor who has worked in schools and now works for a local authority. For the past fifteen years, we have been involved with a community-based support network for mixed race families, which has provided information, support, and advice for parents, as well as participation in research projects and organizing conferences on mixed race people. Over the years, we have become aware of the increasing diversity of mixed families, many of whom have developed national, local, or internet networks.

The term "mixed race"—what does it mean?

Mixed race can be described as people whose parentage is of two or more "races", although race itself is a social construction, a category not based on fact or biology, but based on the need for society to find a way of categorizing people (Tizard & Phoenix, 2002).

Western ideology places a great importance on the notion of an individual, non-differentiated self, which is an essentialist view. Within this ideology, ideas of differentiated "race" are defined as binary opposites, for example, black/white, which suggests that people have unchanging, fixed identities. It is within these constructions that people of mixed race are perceived as being "between two cultures", or "neither one thing nor another", thus creating an either/or identity (*ibid.*). Obama's reference to his decision not to refer to his mother's race in order to fit in is an example of the either/or identity.

Mixed race identity

Social constructionism posits that we move away from taken for granted realities and consider the ways in which identities are socially produced. Identity is not simply one thing for an individual; each individual is located in, and opts for differing, and at times, conflictual identities, depending on the social, political, economic, and ideological aspects of their situation, which change over time. Within this ideology, we can no longer think of black and white people as binary opposites. We use the term "racialization" to include ideas that "racial meanings are not static but are socially constructed and dynamic social processes" (*ibid.*, personal communication, Phoenix, 2002). We find this a useful way of conceptualizing mixed racedness because it permits descriptions of the complexity of cultural and racial mixes.

Language

The language used to describe mixed race people is varied and includes: mixed race, mixed heritage, mixed parentage, mestizo, mestiza, mulatto, creole, coloured, mixed racial descent, mixed origins, dual heritage, dual parentage, multi-racial, bi-racial, multi-ethnic, to more derogatory terms such as: half-caste, zebra, half-breed, mongrel, oreo (Ifekwunigwe, 1999). These terms are used in the USA and in the UK, but in other cultures, people of mixed heritage are referred to in various ways: for example, in Japan, people of Japanese and non-Japanese heritages are called "Hafu", which means half-Japanese, and are a distinctive group in a predominantly mono-ethnic culture in which their non-Japanese cultural heritages are less recognized and acknowledged.

Current research on preferences for terminology and classification of mixed heritage (in preparation for the 2011 Census) among mixed heritage peoples inform us of the extent to which descriptions are multiple and complex. Findings based on forty-seven responses to questionnaires about categories and terminology show us the varied and detailed responses, such as, "my mother is Italian and my father is Iranian; my mother is a UK born Muslim of Irish (mother) and Pakistani (father) parentage" (Aspinall, Song, & Hashem, 2006). The research also explored responses to terminology and found that the mixed heritage participants considered the term "Dual heritage" offensive. The reason given is "Many of us are more than dual". Half-caste was regarded as pejorative, "because it sounds derogatory", and "because it portrays the notion that I am only half a person" (*ibid.*, p 16).

Here in the UK, debates continue with mixed race peoples about the preferences on terminology.

History

Mixing between races, particularly between black and white, has had a troubled history. Scientists of the late nineteenth and early twentieth centuries suggested that mixed unions would create "hybrid degeneration", that is mental, physical, and emotional deformities, a sense of whiteness being contaminated with black blood. Although these views were discredited by scientists by the mid-twentieth century, the idea of mixed race people having a problematic identity continued.

The rule of "hypodescent" was introduced in the USA to prevent or limit black and white mixing. The rule was that individuals whose lineages are both white and non-white were categorized within the non-white group, resulting in racial mixing occurring only within black groups, leaving white groups as "pure". However, a significant proportion of individuals who identify themselves as white have multicultural origins (Pinderhughes, 1995).

Demographics

The Census of 2001 had, for the first time, included the category of mixed parentage, and showed that Britain has the highest rate of inter-ethnic relationships in the west. A recent MORI survey confirms that that there are relatively high levels of social interaction between races, with 70% claiming that they are comfortable for their children to choose a partner of a different race or faith (Platt, 2009). The mixed heritage population is now the third largest ethnic minority group, and is set to become the biggest over the next decade. More than half of the mixed heritage population is under sixteen years, and one in four children of the mixed race population is under five years of age.

It is problematic to refer to mixed race people as the single largest minority group, as there are other significant factors of differentiation, such as class and region, to consider.

Research on mixed-race couples and families

There has been increased research on people of mixed parentage, or "insider accounts". Some research has focused on mixed race adults (Ifekwunigwe, 1999; Korgen, 1998; Olumide, 2002; Root, 1996; Spickard, 1989), while others have focused on mixed race relationships (Killian, 2001; Luke & Luke, 1999).

Caballero, Edward, and Puthussery (2006) explored the everyday lives of mixed heritage, mixed faith families and found varied responses to parental negotiations of belonging and difference. Some parents did not encourage their children to locate their identities within either one culture or another and had the idea of being "open" to both. Others promoted the idea of belonging to one culture.

Sims' research with British–Thai families confirms the relevance and importance of location and forms of support. She found that with some families, fluency in the Thai language could not be sustained because of a lack of Thai speakers in their area. The establishment of local support networks, such as Thai supplementary schools or a temple, provided important social interactions with other Thai and mixed families (Sims, 2007).

Tikly, Caballero, Haynes, and Hill (2004), within an educational setting, found that teachers had assumptions of mixed race pupils experiencing identity problems, although positive images of mixed identities occurred at home. Teachers expressed some uncertainty about the correct terminology to use with mixed heritage pupils, and to avoid using the "wrong" term, mixed heritage pupils were subsumed under the category of African Caribbean. These assumptions of terminology may lead to a lack of understanding by some professionals regarding the complexity of mixing of children and their families.

Conclusion

From the above brief introduction, it is clear that although there has been a fair amount of research and thinking about mixed race heritage populations, there has not been a corresponding amount of training in this area. Professionals working with children, young people, adults, and their families, in diverse contexts, for example, in schools or social care settings, may not be aware of the issues relevant to those who are from mixed heritage backgrounds. The exercises that follow are an attempt to bridge this gap by raising awareness about mixed race heritage people.

References

Aspinall, P., Song, M., & Hashem, F. (2006). *Mixed Race in Britain: Interim Report*. Canterbury: University of Kent.

Caballero, C., Edward, R., & Puthussery, S. (2006). Parenting "mixed" children: negotiating difference and belonging in mixed race, ethnicity and faith families. London: Joseph Rowntree Foundation.

Ifekwunigwe, J. (1999). *Scattered Belongings: Cultural Paradoxes of "Race", Nation and Culture*. London: Routledge.

Killian, K. D. (2001). Dominant and marginalized discourses in interracial couples' narratives: implications for family therapists. *Family Process, 41*(4): 603–618.

Korgen, K. (1998). *From Black to Biracial: Transforming Racial Identity Among Americans*. Westport, CT: Praeger.

Luke, C., & Luke, A. (1999). Interracial families: difference within difference. *Ethnic and Racial Studies, 21*(4): 728–755.

Obama, B. (2007). *Dreams of my Father*. Edinburgh: Canongate.

Olumide, J. (2002). *Raiding the Gene Pool*. London: Pluto Press.

Pinderhughes, E. (1995). Biracial identity: asset or handicap? In: W. W. Harris, H. C. Blue & E. E. H. Griffiths (Eds), *Racial and Ethnic Identity. Psychological Development and Creative Expression* (pp. 73–93). New York: Routledge.

Platt, L. (2009). *Ethnicity and Family. Relationships within and between ethnic groups: An Analysis Using the Labour Force Survey.* Colchester: University of Essex: Institute for Social and Economic Research.

Root, M. (1996). The multiracial experience: racial borders as a significant frontier in race relations. In: M. Root (Ed.), *The Multiracial Experience: Racial Borders as the New Frontier* (p. xiii). Thousand Oaks, CA: Sage.

Sims, J. (2007). Thai–British families: towards a deeper understanding of "mixedness". CRE Conference 4–6 September.

Spickard, P. (1989). *Mixed Blood*. Madison City: University of Wisconsin Press.

Tikly, L. Caballero, C., Haynes, J., & Hill, J. (2004). *Understanding the Needs of Mixed Heritage Pupils*. London: DfES.

Tizard, B., & Phoenix, A. (2002). *Black, White or Mixed Race?* London: Routledge.

The Wordz Out (2005). DVD. Nottingham City Museum and Galleries.

Exercises

Exercise 1: Who do I think you are?

Aims

- To demonstrate the complexity and diversity of culture.
- To demonstrate the extent to which judgements and categories are defined on the basis of skin colour, name, accents.
- To discuss ways in which assumptions can be questioned.

Instructions

Participants: 10–14; total time: 40–45 mins; resources: flipchart, pens.

1. Introduce yourself (the trainer) by name only; do not introduce the rest of the group (2 mins).
2. Split the group into pairs (5 mins).
3. Ask the pairs to interview each other in turn by guessing the culture, race, or ethnicity of their partner. They then discuss what thoughts had come up for each other, check the responses of each other, for example, was this experience different from others? (20 mins).

4. The whole group comes back together to discuss their experiences (10 mins).

Notes for trainers

●   This exercise can evoke apprehension and anxiety and elicit a range of emotions that need to be skilfully facilitated and processed.
●   Refer to the importance of having these conversations with clients.
●   This exercise could be used fairly early on in training, or with a relatively new group, who do not yet know each other's racial/ethnic backgrounds.

Exercise 2: Using Video

Context/organization

A DVD, *The Wordz Out*, a series of seven short films made by young Black British people in which they explore their aspirations, stereotypes, and racism associated with being young and black. The selected film, *The Grey Area*, explores the experiences of two mixed race young women who talk of the names others used to describe them, such as "half-caste", "half-breed", negative comments from both black and white people, and their experiences of having to choose one identity over another. The girls describe how their cultural knowledge and practices of music, hair care, and use of language were questioned by black peers in order to identify them.

Aims

●   For the participants to hear "insider accounts" of the experiences of being mixed race.
●   To gain knowledge of how young mixed race people experience and respond to assumptions made about them.
●   To increase awareness that such conversations are part of their everyday lives.

Instructions

Participants: 10–12; total time: 45 mins (more if the group is larger); resources: flipchart

1. Split the group into threes/fours (5 mins).
2. One person in each group is assigned the task of interviewing another member of the group while the other (two) observe (10 mins).
3. The questions could include:
    ●   What was their initial response to the DVD?
    ●   Did it provide any new information for them?

- Were there ideas that they were most/least connected to?
- How would they think about working with a young mixed race person who told them of these experiences?

4. Ask the small groups to reconvene in the larger group.
5. The interviewees are first asked to share their experience of being interviewed, followed by the interviewers (10 mins).
6. The observers finally discuss their reflections and observations (10 mins).
7. Final large group discussion (10 mins).

Notes for trainers

- There may be different generational responses from older professionals and from young people.
- It can be helpful to spend some time connecting the ideas raised by the exercise to practice.

Exercise 3: Mixed relationships (1)

Context

Developed from Nick Banks (1996).

Aims

- To raise awareness of perceptions of mixed relationships.
- To consider one's own position in relation to mixed relationships.
- To enable professionals to discuss cultural mixing of clients.

Instructions

Participants: 12–15; total time: between one and one and half hours; resources: sheets with typed questions, flipchart paper.

1. Divide the group into threes. One person is the interviewer, one the interviewee, and one the observer. The observer's role is to ascribe the main points and feed back to the larger group. Flipchart paper and a list of questions is handed to each group (10 mins).
2. A series of questions is then put to the interviewee to stimulate a discussion on cultural mixing (20 mins).
    The questions are as follows:
    - What is your view of mixed relationships and/or mixed heritage children?
    - Is there any cultural mixing in your family?
    - What messages did you receive about mixed race relationships when you were growing up?

- What stories did you hear?
- What are society's views of mixed heritage people?
- How do you explain your view in relation to society's view?
- Do you work with mixed heritage children and/or families?
- What, do you think, are the issues for mixed heritage families and/children?
- How has this affected your work as a professional?
3. Each group feeds back to the larger group (30 mins).

Notes for trainers

- This can be a challenging exercise for participants, so a safe learning context needs to be established before the introduction of this exercise.
- Awareness of the process of participants responding to questions is important, and you may need to consider how you pace this exercise: for example, selection of two questions could enable greater self reflexivity.
- You will also need to consider the racial and cultural mix of the group and ensure that there is a balance of respondents' ethnicities in the exercise.

Reference

Banks, N. (1996). Young single white mothers with black children. *Clinical Psychology and Psychiatry*, *1*(1): 19–28.

Exercise 4: Mixed relationships (2)

Aims

- To raise awareness of perceptions of mixed relationships.
- To consider one's own position in relation to mixed relationships.
- To enable professionals to discuss cultural mixing with clients.

Instructions

Participants: 10–14; total time: approximately one hour; resources: sheets of paper to write on, pens, and a box to place papers in.

1. Participants are asked to write a couple of sentences about mixed relationships and mixed heritage children in answer to the questions as follows (10 mins).

Questions:

- What is your view of mixed relationships and/or mixed heritage children?
- Is there any cultural mixing in your family?
- Are there different views about this in your family?
- What are society's views of mixed heritage people?
- How do you explain your view in relation to society's view?
- Do you work with mixed heritage children and/or families?
- What, do you think, are the issues for mixed heritage families and/children?
- How has this affected your work as a professional?

2. After a couple of questions, people are asked to fold up their sheets of paper with their ideas and place it in a box in the middle of the group. They are then asked to divide into groups of two or three. One member of each group selects one piece of paper from the box, returns to their group, and discusses the written statements (15–20 mins).

3. The large group comes together to share their understandings about mixed relationships and reflect upon the process of doing the exercise (30 mins).

Notes for trainers

This is an interesting exercise, which can get the group to work with people they may not know very well and to learn about each other's ways of working.

Exercise 5: Being privileged, whether you know it or not.

Context

Developed from REWIND, a project located within Oldbury and Smethwick Primary Care Trust.

Aim

To increase awareness of the effects of stereotypes in society.

Instruction

Participants: between 3 and 12; total time: approximately one hour; resources: flipchart paper, pens.

1. Hand out sheets of paper with a series of questions which the participants answer individually, as follows (20 mins).

- Name all the stereotypes about different groups of people. Are you among one of the groups that have many stereotypes about them?
- Make a list of the derogatory names that are made towards people of different colours, sexual orientation, abilities, gender.
- When completing ethnic monitoring questionnaires, is there a category that matches how you would describe yourself?
- Did you study the writing or books of people who were the same colour as you in school?
- If you were born in this country, has your Britishness or your right to be in your home country ever been questioned?

2. Upon completion, the participants are divided into groups of two or three to discuss their experience of completion of the questions (15 mins).
3. The facilitator takes the feedback from the whole group and writes it up on the flipchart (10 mins).
4. The participants reflect upon their experience of doing the exercise (10 mins).

Notes for trainers

- This can be a challenging exercise for participants so a safe learning context needs to be established before the introduction of this exercise.
- Awareness of the process of participants responding to questions is important, and you may need to consider how you pace this exercise, for example, selection of two questions could enable greater self reflexivity.
- You will also need to consider the racial and cultural mix of the group and ensure that there is a balance of respondents' ethnicities in the exercise.

B. Working with intercultural couples

Reenee Singh and Sumita Dutta

In the previous section, Yvonne Ayo and Melanie Gabbi discussed the issues for mixed race heritage children, young people, and their families. In this section, we will focus more specifically on the couple/parenting subsystem within such families.

Who is this section for?

This section is aimed most directly at training couple counsellors. However, it is also relevant for those working with individuals and families, as couple issues often emerge as part of the work with individuals and families. For example, if you are training those working in school settings, they might receive a referral for a child who is refusing to attend school. If and when the school professional convenes a family meeting, she might find that the child is staying at home to protect his parents from their conflicts with each other.

What do we mean by intercultural couples?

Although the title refers to intercultural couples, by which we mean couples who are from different cultural backgrounds, the issues relate to *all* couples, regardless of their racial and ethnic origins. If we think of culture as fluid, shifting, and dynamic (Krause & Miller, 1995) differences between people of a similar cultural background may be as difficult to negotiate as differences between people of very dissimilar cultural backgrounds. For example, in the Indian subcontinent, there may be vast differences between a Punjabi man and a woman from Kerala with regard to their diet, child rearing practices, and cultural beliefs and values. This may be the case despite the fact that both are "Indian" and belong to the same class and religious background. Similarly, a woman from the north of the UK may experience her culture as profoundly different from a man who has always lived in London, although they might both define themselves as white English or white British.

We believe that the establishment of any couple relationship requires a negotiation of differences—in areas such as how festivals are celebrated, what kind of food is eaten, relationships with families of origin, and rules about bringing up children.

Step families or reconstituted families provide one instance of highlighting difference; when couples bring children from previous relationships into a new relationship, the process of negotiating difference also applies to children, who might have different sets of rules in the different households that they belong to (Gorrell Barnes, 1998). Working with intercultural or interfaith couples is yet another instance of a more *explicit* process of negotiating differences. Although, thus far, we have referred to heterosexual couples, the issues raised in this section also apply to same sex couples. For the purposes of this section, we will refer to intercultural and interfaith couples interchangeably, as we believe that there is considerable overlap in the issues for couples from either different cultural or different religious backgrounds.

If, as we have argued, being in any couple relationship entails a negotiation of differences, what might be the issues more specific to intercultural or interfaith couples? We will now discuss a few themes that, in our experience, cut across our work with intercultural couples.

Transitions and change

Although life cycle or developmental changes may be challenging for any couple and family, perhaps the differences become particularly pronounced when the couple is from different cultural and religious backgrounds. Carter and McGoldrick (1989) point out that negotiating changes in the family life cycle is often done in reference to, and in support with, the cultural and community resources available to people. For example, a child is marked as coming into the world in various ceremonies, such as a christening or a "mundan" (a Hindu ceremony). Similarly, some cultures mark the move into adolescence through ceremonies such as the Jewish celebration of a Bar Mitzvah. When there are competing ideas within the wider family and community networks about which developmental stage should be privileged, and in what ways, this can sometimes lead to conflict.

Similarly, when there are two faiths, sometimes one partner in a couple is forced to let go of their faith in order to be accepted by the other person's community. This can be a very painful loss that may or may not be fully acknowledged in the relationship. In our experience, we have heard from people about how difficult it can be to be absent from religious celebrations, as it as a reminder of the loss of their first religion. Equally, people have talked about the problem of feeling that they do not have agency to pick and choose which aspects of the second religion they would like to take on for themselves.

Migration, loss, and cut-offs

Stories from one or both partners of an intercultural couple often include a description of losses. Sometimes the losses are in previous generations, like the loss of home for migrant and refugee families (Falicov, 1995). Sometimes, marrying outside of one's faith or culture can also involve a loss of relationships with one or both partners' parents or siblings. Such cut-offs can be extremely painful, and come to the fore during the celebration of festivals or rituals, like marriage and childbirth. An exploration of these migration histories and losses can be a very useful way to understand the lived experiences of intercultural couples. In our experience, although this work has to be carried out sensitively and with caution, couples often feel more able to face current dilemmas and negotiations once they feel that their own earlier experiences have been taken into account.

The impact of global conflict

In the case of a couple that I (RS) once worked with, where the husband (Ahmed) was Algerian Muslim and the wife (Pat) was Australian Christian (the couple's names have been altered to protect confidentiality), they found themselves distanced from both their families. Pat's family viewed Ahmed's Muslim background with suspicion, and, despite the fact that Pat had converted to Islam; she was never fully accepted by her husband's family. They had met at a time before the terrible happenings of 9/11 in the USA, the Gulf War, and the bombings in London (7 July 2005). The couple and their two children experienced racism and Islamophobia. During one of our sessions, Ahmed and Pat poignantly recounted that they did not like to watch the news on television, as it reminded them of the conflict between the Western world and the Islamic world. If they kept the outside world at bay, they could preserve the idea of their family as a peaceful unit. However, while this strategy protected them at one level, it also isolated them from the rest of the world on another.

Bi-lingualism

When Pat and Ahmed first met, they spoke to each other in French, in which they were both fluent. However, after they had children, Ahmed wanted to bring up his children to speak Arabic. The language spoken at home thus excluded Pat, who had imagined, before the children were born, that their family life would be conducted in French. Burck (2005) writes about the dilemmas for couples, parents, and families of living in different languages. Language can be used in couple relationships to regulate distance and closeness and to mark power differences.

Second and third generation migrants will often talk about the imbalance in their couple relationships where one member of the couple is from the dominant culture. The one from the minority culture is already subsumed within the dominant language, which means that the minority language has to be introduced in an explicit way, often with the dominant partner having to opt to learn their partner's language. This puts the onus on the minority partner to persuade the other partner to preserve their own language, hence aspects of their own culture.

Rules about bringing up children

Rules about how children should be brought up may vary from one culture to another. Although there is, of course, much intracultural variation as well, with rules about parenting differing between one family and another *within* the *same* cultural background, there may be some marked differences that could be based on cultural and class differences. In some cultures, for example, it is the norm for children to sleep with their parents or in their parents' room, whereas in other cultures, such a practice would be frowned upon.

Sometimes, conflicts or disagreements between intercultural couples focus less on the differences in the rules and more in the way such rules can acquire racial/cultural significance. For example, in my own family, I (RS) am South Asian, married to a white Englishman. Our three-year-old son is mixed race. Recently, when we were on holiday with my mother-in-law, I bumped up against differences in my own and my mother-in-law's ideas about how children should behave in public. My own view is that children should be quiet and well behaved when they are in public places like restaurants, whereas my mother-in-law is of the belief that "boys will be boys" and should be allowed to express themselves through physical activity, despite the context. Following a disagreement between us, when I unpacked these two differing sets of beliefs further, I realised that when my son misbehaved (from my point of view) in a public place in a predominantly white area, I felt acutely aware of my own racial and cultural background as a black person and how this might affect others' perceptions of whether I am a good enough parent. My expectations from my son may be different when I am in a situation where I do not stand out as being from a minority ethnic background.

Conclusion

Although working with intercultural couples involves, at many levels, the same processes as when working with monocultural couples, this section outlines particular areas that the professional could focus on. The exercises that follow are intended both as training tools for those training couple counsellors working with intercultural couples, and as tools that could be used in clinical work with intercultural/interfaith couples.

References

Burck, C. (2005). *Multilingual Living. Explorations of Subjectivity*. London: Routledge.

Carter, E., & McGoldrick, M. (1989). *The Family Life Cycle: A Framework for Family Therapy*. New York: Gardner Press.

Gorrell Barnes, G. (1998). *Family Therapy in Changing Times*. London: Macmillan.

Krause, I. B., & Miller, A. (1995). Culture and family therapy. In: S. Fernando (Ed.), *Mental Health in a Multi-ethnic Society: A Multidisciplinary Handbook* (pp. 149–171). London: Routledge.

Falicov, C. (1995). Training to think culturally: a multidimensional comparative framework. *Family Process, 34*: 389–399.

Exercises

Exercise 1: Couple cultural genograms

Context/organization

This exercise was devised by Reenee Singh, adapted from Hardy and Laszloffy's (1995) Cultural Genogram (p. 33). It can be used in clinical intercultural work, as well as to train professionals.

Aims

● To encourage participants to think about the cultural influences in their own families of origin.

- To help participants to understand how one's own cultural background may differ from one's partner.
- To help participants learn how to negotiate cultural differences in a couple relationship.

Instructions

Particpants: between 4 and 16 (even numbers required); total time: approximately two and half hours; resources: flipchart paper, coloured pens/pencils, handouts with typed questions.

1. Break the group into pairs. Spread them across the room, or, ideally, in break-out rooms attached to the main training room (5 mins).
2. Provide each pair with a piece of flipchart paper and coloured pens/pencils (5 mins).
3. Ask one person to help the other to draw their own cultural genogram/family tree of three generations and then that of their partner's. Direct participants to use colours to identify different cultural backgrounds within their own family and that of their partner's family (45 mins).
4. After the families have been mapped out, ask each pair to reflect upon the following questions. How are the two genograms similar and different? What is the impact of cultural, faith, and language differences on parenting? How were intercultural/interfaith differences negotiated in their own and their partners' families as they were growing up? In their couple relationships, what patterns and themes about cultural/faith difference do they think they have adopted/changed from their own and from their partners' families (30 mins)?
5. Break: pairs should now swap over and repeat the above stages (45 mins).
6. Once both people in the pairs have had a chance to be interviewed, bring the large group back together and ask them to reflect upon the process of doing the exercise and reflect together on the main learning points (20 mins).

Notes for trainers

- This is a long and complex exercise, best suited for professionals who already have experience in drawing genograms and cultural genograms.
- Those who do not have a current partner could be asked to think about a previous relationship.
- When participants and their partners are from what they would consider to be monocultural and unifaith backgrounds, they may be

encouraged to think about culture in its broadest sense, as encompassing differences in class and place.

●   This exercise could evoke strong feelings about the participants' family and couple relationships, and you should allow space for participants to approach you and talk in private, if necessary.

●   It is important that you let people know at the start of the exercise that they will not be expected to share details of their discussion in the large group and that they can take away their genograms at the end of the session.

Exercise 2: Couple multi-dimensional ecological comparative analysis (MECA).

Context/organization

This exercise was devised by Reenee Singh, based on Falicov's (1995) MECA framework.

Aim

To help participants to explore the differences between couples, using Falicov's (1995) MECA as a framework.

Instructions

Participants: 8–24; duration: approximately one and a half hours; resources: handouts with descriptions of Falicov's four MECA parameters.

1.   Briefly summarize each of the parameters of Falicov's MECA (p. 14) (10 mins).
     ●   Ecological context.
     ●   Migration/acculturation.
     ●   Family life cycle.
     ●   Family organization.

2.   Break the group into pairs (5 mins) and spread them out across the room. Ask each pair to assign roles of interviewer and interviewee.

3.   Explain to the group that they can choose one of Falicov's four parameters to think about in more detail. The trainer should try to ensure that all parameters are covered among the pairs, if possible.

4.   Once each pair has been assigned a parameter, they are given a further handout with a description of their parameter and an opportunity to clarify any further aspects of Falicov's model (5 mins).

5,   Using the assigned parameter, the interviewer asks the interviewee to consider what connections they make to the parameter from the position of

      (a) their own growing up and family of origin;

      (b) their partner's growing up and family of origin (20 mins).

6.   After twenty minutes, ask the pairs to switch roles and repeat the above stages (20 mins).

7.   Bring the pairs back into the large group and ask people to reflect upon some of the couple differences/similarities that emerged, in a way that they feel comfortable sharing (15 mins).

Notes for trainers

- This exercise relies on a previous theoretical discussion (p. 14) that includes the idea of Falicov's (1995) MECA as a training tool (14 mins).
- This exercise could evoke strong feelings about the participants' family and couple relationships and you should allow space for participants to approach you and talk in private, if necessary.

Exercise 3: Mind your language

Context/organization

This exercise was devised by Reenee Singh, based on Charlotte Burck's (2005) research on multilingualism.

Aims

- To help participants to reflect on how differences in languages between any two people can be negotiated.
- To facilitate an awareness about the richness and strengths in being able to speak in more than one language.

Instructions

Participants: 2–12; duration: between an hour and hour and half; resources: handouts with typed questions.

1.   Break the group into pairs (5 mins).

2.   Ask them to interview each other in turn with regard to the following questions (40 mins):

- When you were growing up, what language(s) were spoken at home?
- If your parents/carers came from different language backgrounds, how were decisions made about what language(s) should be spoken and in what contexts?
- In your current family situation, what language(s) are spoken and when?

- If you speak in more than one language, what is it like for you to switch from one language to another?
- What do you think might be the advantages/disadvantages of speaking more than one language?

3, Ask the pairs to reconvene in the large group (2 mins).

4. Ask the group for feedback about what the process of doing the exercise was like for them, and how it might translate back into their work with bilingual and multilingual couples (15–20 mins).

Notes for trainers

- When introducing the exercise, you should let participants know that you are referring to language in the broadest sense. Language can include differences in dialect, in accents, and even sign language.
- Doing this exercise can bring up strong feelings of loss, particularly if languages (and, by implication, culture and class) have been adapted or lost over generations. You should allow enough time for the last part of the exercise, where you enquire about the process of doing the exercise.

Exercise 4: East is East

Context/organization

This exercise was devised by Reenee Singh.

Aims

- To help professionals to think about how cultural and religious differences are managed in intercultural and interfaith couple relationships.
- To think about the impact of these differences on parenting.

Instructions

Participants: 3–50; total time: 30–45 mins; resources: DVD, DVD player, flipchart paper, handouts.

1. Advise participants that you are going to show them a clip from a film.
2. Ask them to bear the following questions in mind as they are watching it (you may want to have these questions on flipchart/handouts).
    - What cultural and faith differences do you notice?
    - How are these differences managed and negotiated in the couple relationship?
    - What is the impact of these parenting differences on the children's mixed race identities?
3. Now show the participants a ten-minute clip from the film *East is East*, (This is a BAFTA Award winning British comedy drama, directed by

Damien O'Donnell and released in 1999. It is based in Britain in the 1970s and is a poignant exposition of the dilemmas faced by a mixed race family, where the father is Pakistani Muslim and the mother is English, of Irish Catholic origin.)

4. Now ask the group to reflect upon what they have seen. This can either be in pairs or as a large group. Ask people to also consider the impact that the film clip has had on them. If this reflection is done in pairs, then bring the group back together and ask participants to share some of their reflections in pairs with the large group, making sure that each of the questions are covered.

Notes for trainers

● You could substitute the film *East is East* with another film about inter-cultural couple relationships.

● Rather than asking individuals to cover all three questions, you could break the group into two and ask Group 1: What cultural and faith differences do you notice and how do these get managed and negoti-ated in the couple relationship? Group 2 could be asked: What is the impact of parenting differences on the children's mixed race identities? Discussion and feedback as per above.

● In one of the training groups that I (RS) facilitated, a Muslim participant objected to the way in which his religion was represented in the film. You may want to allow enough time for discussion and debriefing after showing the film, or you may want to check that nobody in the audi-ence has strong feelings about the film before showing it.

Exercise 5: The dinner table

Context/organization

This exercise was devised by Sumita Dutta. It can be used to guide clinical sessions with intercultural couples as well as training professionals.

Aims

● To look at what food is eaten within the home.
● To explore the origins and meanings associated with food from a cultural perspective.
● To consider how what gets eaten in the home is thought about and negotiated.

Instructions

Participants: 4–24 (even numbers required); total time: 45 mins–1 hour (30 mins pair interviewing, 15–30 mins large group feedback); resources: hand-outs with typed questions.

1. Break the group into pairs. Spread them out across the room. Give each pair a handout with the questions that are going to be asked (see questions below).
2. Ask each pair to identify themselves as an interviewer and interviewee.
3. Explain to the group that they will take it in turns to interview each other about the ways in which family meals are thought about and have been experienced in their family of origin.
4. The interviewer is now directed towards asking the following questions around the following areas (as per handout) (15 mins):
    ● What did you eat last night at home?
    ● How did what you eat at home get talked about or negotiated in your partnership/with significant others?
    ● How does this compare to the food that you ate in your family of origin?
    ● Do you make any cultural associations with food?
    ● If your partner/a significant other person to you were here, what would s/he be able to tell me about what cultural associations you have with food?
5. After fifteen minutes, the trainer should direct the pairs to swap over, so the interviewer is now interviewed, and to repeat the above (15 mins).
6. Ask the group to come back together and feed back on the process of the exercise and some of the connections that they made to their own lives and their work with intercultural couples (15–30 mins).

Notes for trainers

It is important to recognize that food or "home food" can be a very evocative subject, with strong emotional and contextual associations with, for example, poverty, racism, or loss. For this reason, I usually leave 15–30 minutes for large group feedback.

Participants have often fed back how useful this exercise is to directly transfer into their work with intercultural couples because of the strong resonances it can create.

Exercise 6: The celebration

Context/organization

This exercise was devised by Sumita Dutta. It can be used to guide clinical sessions with intercultural couples as well as training professionals.

Aims

● To look at what celebrations take place within couple relationships.

- To consider how cultural celebrations and rituals get thought about and negotiated in couples.

Instructions

Participants: 4–24 (even numbers required); total time: 45 mins–1 hour (30 mins pair interviewing, 15–30 mins large group feedback); resources: handouts with typed questions.

1. Break the group into pairs. Spread them out across the room. Give each pair a handout with the questions (see below).
2. Ask each pair to identify themselves as an interviewer and interviewee.
3. Explain to the group that they will take it in turns to interview each other about the ways in which they celebrate festivals or rituals within their couple/family.
4. The interviewer is now directed towards asking the following questions around the following areas (as per handout) (15 mins);
   - What was the last festival that you celebrated together as a couple/family (e.g., Christmas, Divali, etc.).
   - How does this compare to the festivals or rituals that you experienced in your family of origin?
   - How did what you celebrate get talked about or negotiated with in your partnership?
5. After fifteen minutes the trainer should direct the pairs to swap over, so the interviewer is now interviewed and to repeat the above (15 mins).
6. Ask the group to come back together and feed back on the process of the exercise and some of the connections that they made to their own lives and their work with intercultural couples (15–30 mins).

Note for trainers

It is important to recognize that all couples have to negotiate how to do festivals within relationships, even if they are from the same culture. For example, how Christmas gets negotiated in a couple from the same culture can often be very complicated. This is sometimes a nice way to introduce the exercise and connect participants to their own cultural experiences.

Exercise 7: Exploring views on intercultural couples

Context/organization

This exercise was devised by Sumita Dutta.

Aims

- To look at your own views of intercultural couples.
- To consider how these views were influenced.
- To explore the views of people around you on intercultural couples.

Instruction

Participants: 2–24 (even numbers required, ideally); duration: 55 mins–70 mins (40 mins pair interviewing, 15–30 mins large group feedback); resources: handouts with typed questions.

1. Break the group into pairs. Spread them out across the room. Give each pair a handout with the questions that are going to be asked (see questions below).
2. Ask each pair to identify themselves as an interviewer and interviewee.
3. Explain to the group that they will take it in turns to interview each other about their views on intercultural couples.
4. The interviewer is now directed towards asking questions (as per handout) around the following areas (20 mins):
    - What are your own views on intercultural couples? How were these shaped? Did you know any intercultural couples growing up, in your early adulthood, later life? Did any public representations of intercultural couples influencing your views? Did anyone around you have strong views that influenced you?
    - If your partner were here, what would s/he say were their views on intercultural couples? Do you know how these were shaped? Did they know any intercultural couples growing up, in their early adulthood, later life? Did any public representations of intercultural couples influence their views? Did anyone around them have any strong views that influenced them?
    - If your parents/children or significant others from your life were here, what would they say were their views on intercultural couples? Do you know how these were shaped? Did they know any intercultural couples growing up, in their early adulthood, later life? Did any public representations of intercultural couples influence their views? Did anyone around them have any strong views that influenced them?
5. After twenty minutes, the trainer should direct the pairs to swap over, so the interviewer is now interviewed, and to repeat the above (20 mins).
6. Ask the group to come back together and feed back on the process of the exercise and some of the connections that they made to their own lives and their work with intercultural couples (15–30 mins).

Note for trainers

This exercise can bring forth people's own experiences of being discrimi-
nated against, both within their couples and their families of origin. It may
be important to keep some time "in hand" to fully process the exercise, I
usually leave 15–30 minutes for large group feedback, as well as naming
discrimination and racism as an aspect of many intercultural couples' life
experiences.

PART FOUR

Kinship care: working with children

Sara Barratt and Sumita Dutta

Theoretical overview

Who is this chapter for?

This chapter is directed primarily at people working with children looked after by kin, that is, families or friends of their biological parents, but is relevant to anyone working with children who wants to think about cultural transitions and identity.

> Behind my skin
> I cannot even begin
> To express the loss
> The devastating cost of trying to fit in,
> The need to belong.
> How I wish it were gone. [Jardine, 2006]

Kinship care: setting the context

The 1989 Children Act stipulated that, where a child is looked after by the local authority and cannot be placed with parents, priority should be given to placement with members of extended family or social networks. The Act also states that a local authority should give due consideration to the child's religious persuasion, racial origin, and cultural and linguistic background (Children Act, 1989, 22.5). A study by Hunt, Waterhouse, and Lutman (2008, p. 287) found that only one third of kin placements in their sample were instigated by social services. Thus, many kinship placements are private arrangements made between parents, families, and friends.

Brah (1996) proposes that culture should not be viewed as a fixed static entity, but should be conceptualized as a fluid relational process, which is at once influencing and being influenced by the environment. In the context of looked after children, a child's racial and cultural identity is, therefore, viewed as being actively shaped with every new environment and placement the child finds himself in. In this chapter, we explore some of these cultural considerations in the context of kinship care.

In the UK, fifteen per cent of the care population is in kinship placements; this compares with forty per cent in the USA and thirty-five per cent in New Zealand. Within the UK, there are also regional variations. Traditionally, kinship care has been contained within foster care services, so any resources that do exist have been provided in the context of "stranger" foster care services rather than being tailored to the more specialist needs of kinship care services. In his study, Broad (1998) found that 58% of his sample of children in kinship care were black or of mixed ethnicity.

Boyd-Franklin and Bry (2000) highlight the importance of extended family networks when working with black and minority ethnic children. Children from minority ethnic backgrounds often have multiple attachments to extended family members. For children who are placed with families or friends, there is a stronger possibility that they will live with someone who is from a similar cultural background to that of their biological parents.

Racial identity is relevant to all children, whether black or white. Culture, religion, and language are three distinct elements of identity that interconnect with racial and ethnic identity. For example, a child can be born into a family with one cultural background, speak one language, and be brought up with a particular set of religious beliefs. With a change of lifestyle, a new parental partnership, or a geographical move, some or all of these aspects of a child's life may change, while their racial and ethnic identity remains the same.

One in five children in the UK for whom adoption is the plan comes from black or minority ethnic groups (Performance Innovation Unit, 2000). Harris (2005) says that black parents are excluded from adoption support services, which will affect the contact arrangements between them and their biological children. People are motivated to become adopters because they want to create a family of their own; they often resent the expectation that a child should have contact, whether by letter or face to face, with members of their extended families. This makes it harder for them to really help a child hold on to his/her racial and cultural identity. Thus, for biological parents, there is a stronger possibility that they will remain in touch with their children if they are cared for by families or friends.

Children may be looked after by kinship carers either under a residence order, as foster carers, or, more commonly, in recent years, as special guardians. A study by Farmer and Moyers (2008), comparing 142 kinship care placements with 128 unrelated care placements, found that there was little difference between the two groups in terms of pre-placement difficulties experienced by children and that, on balance, children in kinship placements do at least as well as those placed in unrelated placements. Sinclair, Baker, Lee, and Gibbs (2007) say that foster care by relatives is of lower quality, but is compensated by other factors. Broad and Skinner (2005) indicate that

- kinship care means that the cultural ties and birth identity of the child can be preserved more easily;
- there is more contact with birth parents when children are placed with kinship care. However, the effects of contact, whether good and bad, are amplified with kinship care;
- more children in kinship care described feeling loved than in "stranger" placements. According to Sinclair, Baker, Lee, and Gibbs (2007), if the relationship between the child and the carer is strong and happy, the placement is more likely to work. In "stranger" foster care, this relationship cannot be assessed until after a few months, whereas in kinship placements it can be observed before the placement even starts.

- kinship placements tend to be more stable than "stranger" placements;
- there is no evidence that kinship care is more or less safe than "stranger" placements;
- overall well-being: this is similar with both kinship care and "stranger" foster care in terms of education, health and development, growth, and activities.

The profile of kinship carers is different from other foster carers. They tend to be older and poorer, with more severe health problems. They are also more likely to be single carers.

There are many reasons that children are looked after by people other than their biological parents. These include children who have suffered abuse, abandonment, or neglect, children who have migrated, and children who have been orphaned by tragedy. They may have been born to parents who are drug or alcohol dependent, have mental health problems, or those who are not able to meet their children's needs for a variety of reasons. All of these children experience some sort of cultural bereavement and dislocation. This connects to what Papadopoulos (1997, 2001a,b, 2002), writing in the context of refugee and migration, identifies as "invisible losses". Importantly, these are aspects of everyday life: sounds, smells, temperature, light, music, etc., that one only recognizes as distinct aspects of one's cultural identity once they are lost.

For example, SB worked with a young girl called Amina, who was referred because her foster carer could not manage her behaviour. Amina wanted to live with her half sister, Aziza. The girls came from Somalia, and Amina arrived in the UK when she was five, some time after her elder sister. Neither girl was able to explain how they came to be in the UK, but Aziza, aged nineteen, was applying to care for her half sister against the better judgement of the Social Services department. It was, initially, hard for the girls to speak about their experiences of seeing their parents killed, and of talking about family members they had lost. However, interspersed with these painful memories was talk about shared experience of what their aunt liked to cook. Their memories were of living in very close proximity to members of their family, while the coldness and distance, both physical and emotional, of London was a sharp contrast. As the work progressed, they started to talk about what food they would be able to cook if Social Services agreed that Aziza could become Amina's carer. In time, as they could begin to see a future together, Amina's behaviour was more contained and the work interwove discussions about their traumatic past, their hopes of being reunited with family members, and their plans for a future together, where they could establish their own traditions and re-establish their cultural identity.

One of the key adjustments that mark a child's changes in care and culture is food. In another instance, SB was working with a ten-year-old girl whose family originated in the Caribbean. In her family, she ate traditional food; she then moved to a family which ate junk food, to a relative who did not cook and provided very little food, to another carer who was vegetarian, then to her grand-mother, who gave her traditional food, and so she managed to adjust to the different food that was provided. Each family has its own culture in relation to food, and opening up a talking space with this young girl about food enabled her to talk about some of the difficulties she had faced in adjusting to the patterns of day-to-day life in the different families. Importantly, she relayed how each family thought she should accept the food she was given without question.

Transitions can lead to disconnected stories in relation to family, racial, and ethnic identity. Children and young people will usually come into the care system or be looked after by private arrange-ment. Their carers may be foster carers, members of extended family/friends, or adoptive families following foster care or trans-national adoption. In a birth family, the story of one's cultural iden-tity may be displayed in all sorts of ways. For example, baby photo-graphs on the wall, family pictures depicting place and belonging, regional, cultural, or religious decoration, etc. When children are cared for within kinship placements, some of these aspects of the child's heritage are more likely to be continued, but these will usually be mediated through a filter of what the kinship carer feels is in the best interest of the child. For example, if a child has suf-fered abuse at the hands of one of its parents, this aspect of the child's familial, cultural, and racial history may be minimized and may not be so visible or available to the child for absorption and discussion.

Identity: creating coherent cultural stories

One of the themes in our work is around how to talk to children about their identity and how to manage the child's curiosity or lack of curiosity. It can be more difficult for kinship carers to develop a coherent story of a child's cultural background because they are closely involved with one part of the biological family, have a biased opinion of particular aspects of the child's heritage, or have little knowledge of the other aspects of the child's background. We are aware that sometimes children and carers find it difficult to talk about this because of a conflict of loyalties. There are also times when carers, particularly grandparents, may feel responsible for the lack of care the child has received at the hands of their parents, and this may lead them to minimize the role and influence of the parent's lifestyle as a way of erasing difficult to manage memories. How do we, as professionals, help carers to allow children to be curious about their past?

Professional belief systems

A key consideration appears to be around belonging. To whom does the child belong? How do we help carers and children to open up conversations about their past and about their identity? As professionals, we may have to work with carers to think about their relationship to the looked after child's parents. Children will probably have been abused by a parent and the kinship carer may have ideas about which is the "good"/"bad" family. This can become split along racial lines, and if the child is of mixed heritage, this can add a further dimension of splitting in regards to identity.

Before moving on to look at the exercises, it is important for us to name the cultural influences that we, as professionals, bring to our work with looked after children. We need to be vigilant in our awareness of our own prejudices and blind spots in working with families. Reports into the tragic deaths of children from black and minority ethnic backgrounds cite racism as a powerful element leading to the deaths of children at the hands of their carers. Specific reports (*Whose Child? The Report of the Panel Appointed to Inquire into the Death of Tyra Henry*, London Borough of Lambeth, 1987; *Sukina: An Evaluation of the Circumstances Leading to her Death*, The Bridge Child Care Consultancy Service, 1991; *The Victoria*

Climbié Inquiry, Lord Laming, 2003) make a direct link between the practice of professionals and racist views of professionals when responding to the children and families' concerned. In the Laming report on the death of Victoria Climbié, Graham (2003) says,

> Assumptions based on race can be just as corrosive in its effects as blatant racism . . . racism can affect the way people conduct themselves in other ways. Fear of being accused of racism can stop people acting when otherwise they would . . . It is clear that a more informed approach to the issue of "race" and culture within professional assessment is required. [40: 227].

Our cultural backgrounds determine the attitudes that we have to "good enough" parenting and family life. As professionals, we need to be aware of these organizing principles, which may have a greater influence upon us than our professional belief systems. We need to be aware of the different contexts that influence our definitions of what constitutes good enough parenting and what is in the best interests of a child. Where children are in kinship placements, we may feel less able to challenge unacceptable parenting practices than when a child is placed with related carers. For example, Percy (names and identifying details have been altered to protect confidentiality), who is in his seventies and of Ghanaian origin, is grandfather of two boys for whom he is caring. The boys are active and lively, and Percy keeps a stick by his chair that he uses to discipline the boys. He comes from a culture that says that children should be obedient to their elders and in which physical chastisement is accepted. We worked hard with Percy to try to help him set clearer boundaries for the boys so that the behaviour did not escalate to Percy resorting to the use of physical punishment. Percy did not accept our point of view, and we worked hard, alongside the school and social worker, to help him respond more effectively without violence. For those of us who come from a background where physical chastisement is accepted as good parenting, we may be less likely to challenge Percy's behaviour than if we come from a culture that believes that any physical chastisement is abuse. In our work, it is, therefore, crucial that, as professionals, we have safe and reflective spaces within training and supervision to systematically consider the influence of these cultural beliefs upon the way that we work and listen to accounts of family life.

References

Boyd-Franklin, N., & Bry, B. (2000). *Reaching Out in Family Therapy: Home-based, School and Community Interventions*. New York: Guilford Press.

Brah, A. (1996). *The Cartographies of Diaspora*. London: Routledge.

Broad, B. (1998). *Child Placements with Relatives and Friends Research Project, Final Report*. London: London Borough of Wandsworth Social Services.

Broad, B., & Skinner, A. (2005). *Relative Benefits. Placing Children in Kinship Care*. London: British Association for Adoption and Fostering.

Farmer, E., & Moyers, S. (2008). *Kinship Care: Fostering Effective Families and Friends Placements*. London, Jessica Kingsley.

Graham, N. (QC) (2003). In: *The Victoria Climbié Inquiry: Report of an Inquiry by Lord Laming*. London: The Stationery Office.

Harris, P. (2005). Family is family . . . it does affect everybody in the family: black birth relatives and adoption support. *Adoption and Fostering, 29*(2): 66–75.

Hunt, J., Waterhouse, S., & Lutman, E. (2008). *Keeping It in the Family: Outcomes of Children Placed in Kinship Care through Care Proceedings*. British Association for Adoption and Fostering (BAAF), UK.

Jardine, S. (2006). In my skin (extract). In: P. Harris (Ed.), *In Search of Belonging: Reflections of Transracially Adopted People* (p. 101). London: British Association for Adoption and Fostering.

London Borough of Lambeth (1987). *Whose Child? The Report of the Panel of Inquiry into the Death of Tyra Henry*. London: London Borough of Lambeth.

Papadopoulos, R. K. (1997). Individual identity and collective narratives of conflict. *Harvest: Journal for Jungian Studies, 43*(2): 7–26.

Papadopoulos, R. K. (2001a). Refugees, therapists and trauma: systemic reflections. *Context; The Magazine of the Association for Family Therapy, 54*(April): 5–8. Special issue on Refugees; edited by G. Gorell Barnes & R. K. Papadopoulos.

Papadopoulos, R. K. (2001b). Refugee families: issues of systemic supervision. *Journal of Family Therapy, 23*(4): 405–422.

Papadopoulos, R. K. (2002). Refugees, home and trauma. In: R K. Papadopoulos (Ed.), *Therapeutic Care for Refugees. No Place like Home* (pp. 00–00). London: Karnac.

Performance Innovation Unit (2000). *Prime Minister's Review of Adoption*. Cabinet Office Department of Health.

Sinclair, I., Baker, C., Lee, J., & Gibbs, I. (2007). *The Pursuit of Permanence. A Study of the English Child Care System*. London: Jessica Kingsley.

The Bridge Child Care Consultancy Service (1991). *Sukina: An Evaluation of the Circumstances Leading to her Death*. London: Bridge Child Care Consultancy Service.

Exercises

In the exercises that follow, we explore some of the key cultural themes that arise from considerations of kinship care. In our first exercise, we ask participants to think about what aspects of their own racial and cultural identity is fixed, and what aspects are more transient and malleable to environmental changes. This experiential exercise seeks to connect professionals to ways in which they have been able to negotiate cultural changes as adults in their own lives. They are then asked to reflect upon how these experiences may usefully inform the types of support they think that children might need in negotiating similar cultural changes within placements.

In our second and third exercises, using food as a medium, we explore some of the ways in which cultural rules and norms are identified and negotiated within relationships and families. Thinking about this from a child's perspective, we go on to consider how these experiences may inform our own understanding of the adjustment tasks that children face when they move between homes and communities.

In the fourth exercise, entitled "Children should be seen, not heard . . . and other cultural beliefs", participants are asked to consider what elements of support they were able to draw upon at a time when their own cultural beliefs about child-rearing and family life have been challenged. Participants are encouraged to use their own experiences to consider the types of support that may be helpful to kinship carers when faced with such challenges to their cultural beliefs and practices.

In the final two exercises we look specifically at the way in which cultural identity can be nurtured and sustained at different levels. By asking participants to deconstruct the different ways that their own cultural identities have been formed and constructed (be it in relationships, the family, the school, the community), the exercise seeks to draw out the many different sites of cultural nurturing that exist around children, both in the family and the community.

These then become potential resources for the professional to draw upon to sustain children's cultural identity and create coherent cultural narratives for the child.

Exercise 1: How much do I change?

Context

Developed by Reenee Singh and Sumita Dutta

Aim

To help participants to think about what aspects of their racial and cultural identity are fixed, and what aspects are more transient.

Instructions

Participants: 2+; total time: 40–60 mins.

1. Split the group into pairs (5 mins).
2. Ask each participant to think about a holiday to a foreign country that they remember and then ask each pair to interview each other for about fifteen minutes each around the following questions:
    - What cultural practices in the foreign country did you take on and follow (for example, language, dress, food) and for how long?
    - How many of these were choices? How did it feel if any of these practices did *not* involve you having a choice?
    - While you were following these cultural practices, how did you define your racial/ethnic identity?
3. Feedback about the process and experience of the exercise to the larger group (10 mins).

Notes for trainers

This exercise often connects people to thinking about the levels of choice involved in adopting cultural practices and it is sometimes useful to ask people to connect to their own wider experiences of adaptation and acculturation if people have had experience of migration.

Exercise 2: Family life

Context

Developed by Sara Barratt.

Aims

- To enable participants to consider the assumptions they make about family life.
- To consider the experience of a looked after child.

Instructions

Total time: approximately 30 mins.
In pairs, talk about a time when you went to visit a family member or friend whom you knew slightly.

1. Consider the following:
    (a) What do you remember?
    (b) What were the surprises?
    (c) Were you able to ask questions about food/mealtimes?
    (d) How did you check out the "hidden" rules within the family?
    (e) What did you understand about your cultural beliefs from that experience?
2. Now imagine an eight-year-old child has just come to live in your family.
    (a) What do you think you would need to do to help the child feel at ease?
    (b) What questions do you think the child may have in moving from a family with different cultural practices?

Notes for trainers

This exercise should be undertaken in two stages.

- Part one should be completed before participants are invited to think about the second part of the exercise.
- It is intended to help participants think about their own experience of being in an unfamiliar situation and trying to understand the hidden "rules", and then to think about their own family life and how a child may experience what they would think to be "normal".
- They should be encouraged to think about ways to talk to a child in an unfamiliar environment.

Exercise 3: Food and culture

Context

Developed by Sara Barratt

Aim

To help participants think about the meaning of food in their culture and the relationship between food and identity.

Instructions

Total time: between 30 and 40 mins.

In pairs discuss any or all of the following:

1. Describe the food that was seen as the most enjoyable when you were growing up.
    (a) Do you still eat it?
    (b) What do people you live with/spend time with think about it?
2. Think about a time when you went to eat a meal with a friend and encountered something that you had never seen before.
    (a) What did you do?
3. Think about living with a member of your family where the culture around food is different from your own.
    (a) How may you experience the differences—would it be in relation to smell/ timing/colour/taste/atmosphere/speech?
    (b) How do you think it would be for a child who has moved to live with you?

Note for trainers

Moving between families, even relatives, is always a change of culture, and food is central to our cultural identity. This exercise is intended to help participants look back on their childhood experiences in order to talk to children about the effect of transition, which can be manifested in rituals and the culture of food.

Exercise 4: Children should be seen, not heard . . . and other cultural beliefs

Context/organization

Developed by Reenee Singh and Sumita Dutta

Aim

To help participants understand the connection between beliefs and behaviour regarding child rearing/parenting.

Instructions

Participants: 2+; total time: 45 mins to 1 hour.

1. Split the group into pairs (5 mins).
2. Ask them to interview each other for about twenty minutes each about the following questions:

- Identify three beliefs from your family as you were growing up about how children should be raised, for example the value of education. Further examples could be "work is important", or "children should obey adults".
- Who were the people, experiences, and practices that supported these beliefs in your family or community?
- Now think of a time when one of these beliefs was challenged.
- Who were the people you felt able to speak to about this challenge? What other factors enabled you to consider making a change?

3. Each pair feeds back one or two agreed points from their discussion to the larger group (15 mins).

Note for trainers

Exploring our beliefs about child rearing can evoke strong feelings for participants. It is useful to leave plenty of time for processing in the large group.

Exercise 5: Who am I?

Context

Developed by Reenee Singh and Sumita Dutta

Aim

To help participants to think about how a racial/cultural/ethnic identity can be fostered.

Instructions

Participants: 2+; total time: 1–1.5 hours; resources: a piece of flipchart paper and pens to each pair.

1. Split the group into pairs (5 mins).
2. Ask each pair to interview each other around the following areas (20 mins each):
    (a) When you were growing up, what were the kinds of conversations that your parents/carers had with you about your racial/cultural identity?
      - In what way do you think you developed a sense of racial/cultural identity?
      - Who were the other people and places involved in this development?
      - Were there any questions that you felt you couldn't ask?

    (b) How have your own experiences and sense of racial/cultural iden-
         tity affected the way in which you try to talk to other children (for
         example, in your immediate or extended family) about their racial
         and cultural identities?
    (c) In your professional role, how do you support other people to have
         these conversations with looked after children?

3.   Now distribute flipchart paper and coloured pens to each group and
      ask them to draw a map of the different institutions, resources, people,
      and activities that can be used to develop racial and ethnic identity (10
      mins).

4.   Ask each pair to put their flipchart in the middle of the room and for
      the group to walk round looking at each other's answers (10 mins).

5.   Large group feedback about the process of carrying out the exercise
      and what they noticed from looking at the collated flipcharts (20–30
      mins).

Instructions to trainers

●   It is useful to have the questions on handouts to give each pair.
●   Time keeping is an important aspect of this exercise.
●   Try to carry this exercise out in a room large enough for pairs to have
     privacy in their conversations and for the flipcharts to be put on the
     floor at the end. Alternatively, use Blu-tack and pin them to the wall.
●   The experience of carrying out this exercise is often one that leaves
     participants much more aware of the community resources and insti-
     tutions, such as school, youth clubs, religious and language school
     which promote a child's identity in different ways.

Exercise 6: Coherent stories

Context

Developed by Sara Barratt

Instructions

Participants: 2+; time: 20 mins; resources: pens and paper should be
provided. A genogram should be drawn by the faciltators.

1.   Split participants into groups of four and ask them to consider the
      following scenario.

      A seven-year-old boy has come to live with his maternal grandparents
      following removal from his mother's care because he was found
      wandering the streets looking for help as she was unconscious. The

grandparents are of white/British heritage and the father has been brought up in the UK, but his parents originate in Pakistan. The parents are drug and alcohol dependent, the father is in prison and, following the incident, has been in a rehabilitation centre. The grandparents did not approve of the parents' relationship. The placing social worker is of East African origin and has been working in London for five years.

2.   Ask each participant to take a role of any of the following:
   ● grandfather;
   ● grandmother;
   ● social worker;
   ● child,

   In role, spend five minutes thinking from your perspective about the following questions:
   − What does the child need to know about what is happening to his parents?
   − What questions do you think the child will have about his current situation?
   − What will the child need from you to ensure that he develops a positive sense of his identity?
   − What do you think he should know? What do you think he should not know?

3.   Discuss your answers in the group, with each in turn speaking from his/her perspective (5 mins).

4.   Now coming out of role, what do you, personally, think this child would need from those around him in order to develop a positive view of himself (10 mins)?

5.   The groups should then talk within the larger course group about their experience of this exercise (10 mins).

Notes for trainers

● Trainers can add or subtract family members to ensure that each course participant has a role.
● It would be important for the larger group discussion to think about the way our cultural perspectives influence the way we make decisions in our work and to emphasize the importance of trying to keep the child's experience central.
● Do remember to de-role the participants.

PART FIVE

Positive practices around "race" and culture

Reenee Singh and Sumita Dutta
(Contributors: Jocelyn Avigad, Enid Colmer,
Claire Dempster, Barry Mason, Barbara McKay, and
Amal Treacher)

Theoretical overview

Context

Some of the ideas that this section is based on emerged from the experience of setting up The Centre for Cross-Cultural Studies at the Institute of Family Therapy in 2006. The centre, funded by Lloyds TSB Foundation, was set up by Barry Mason, who was then Director of the Institute of Family Therapy, and staffed by Reenee Singh (Director of the Centre), Sumita Dutta (Systemic Psychotherapist) and Ingrid Mayagibo (Centre Administrator). The members of the Steering Group were Jocelyn Avigad (Chair, Medical Foundation), Amal Treacher (University of Nottingham), Kajetan Kasinski (Tavistock Centre), and Reenee Singh. Although each of the members was clearly committed to the task of setting up the centre, consolidating this commitment proved to be a challenge. Two main aspects that presented as challenging and troublesome were the steering groups' own group processes and the status conferred to the Centre within the wider organizational context. Although it could be argued that any group set up to deal with marginalized populations may have similar experiences, we would like to suggest that perhaps these experiences are even more pronounced when addressing issues of "race" and culture. This may be, in part, because racial and ethnic backgrounds constitute a large part of any person's identity. In any encounter or interchange between two or more people from different—or, indeed, similar racial/cultural backgrounds—differences of "race" and culture and any other kind of differences can thus become polarized.

Approaches and practices

In our history of delivering training, we are aware that participants are keen to dedicate time to thinking about the ways in which to translate ideas from training into practice. The questions of how we transpose some of the ideas outlined so far in this book into our work contexts, and where we find a starting point to open up these discussions, are addressed in this section.

In our experience of working in various outreach, voluntary, and statutory contexts, we have come across different models of incorporating positive approaches to, and practices around, "race" and culture. In this section, we will draw upon our discussions with managers who kindly shared their approaches to working with "race" and culture with us. We will outline some key practices used in organizational contexts. In keeping with the rest of the book, we will present a few exercises that we have devised or adapted for working in organizations.

Who is this section for?

This section is primarily for managers and supervisors, but will be of interest to anyone who wants to think about a range of positive work practices around "race" and culture.

Approaches

In our experience, we have heard managers and supervisors talk about the positive impact that a leader within an organization can have by adopting personal and organizational approaches that

1.   are not afraid to talk about race and culture at work;
2.   recognize power differences and take the lead around diversity issues;
3.   home in on race and culture differences.

Enid Colmer is the past Director of the Centre for Cross-Cultural Studies at the Institute of Family Therapy. Here she reflects her thinking about how to manage staff conflict around differences in teams. She writes about how she considers the

> ways in which power relationships become constructed within teams and how these might interact with the dominant discourses in society that privilege white people and white culture. I am also aware of my own position as a white woman in a senior position in the service . . . I have found Fredman's (1997) ideas about talking about talking useful both in creating a context in which sensitive matters can be discussed respectfully and in setting a neutral stance about whether or not this would be helpful. [Email communication, October 2008]

Here, Colmer is advocating an approach to opening out conversations around race, culture, power, and discrimination in a way that feels safe for people to participate in. Of course, this includes tackling issues of discrimination head on, including accessing organizational complaints' procedures if necessary.

Barabara McKay is the Director of the Institute of Family Therapy. She reflects,

> I suggest that managers or colleagues create a context of curiosity about one another at the level of relational reflexivity. By that I mean develop the skill to ask questions at a relational level such as: "Knowing we are from different cultural contexts, what, if anything, do you think I need to know about you in context that will help me to know how to conduct myself in this conversation?" or "What can I tell you about me that would help us to be attentive to one another in a way that creates an atmosphere of mutual respect and collaboration in this relationship?"
>
> I also need to be mindful that as a manager, in a position of authority, I may inadvertently marginalize other voices or not be sufficiently attentive to the cultural stories around speaking in meetings or in other situations . . . [Email communication, November 2008]

Here, McKay is privileging and awareness of her own power over her colleagues which may make it difficult for others to initiate talking about difference. She is coming from a position of genuine curiosity about the cultural experiences that people bring with them to the workplace and is mindful of the need to negotiate difference. not only in every relationship. but also in every conversation and exchange.

Reenee Singh is the Founding Director of the Centre for Cross-Cultural Studies at the Institute of Family Therapy and currently a Consultant Systemic Psychotherapist at the Tavistock Centre. Her approach to thinking about issues of "race" and culture in an organization is to

> Take a risk in bringing up racialised remarks, comments and incidents as and when they occur. Sometimes people try to be so politically correct that they shy away from taking up such comments or interchanges. As a black person in a position of authority or seniority in predominantly white organisations, I sometimes feel as if I am positioned to speak on behalf of *all* my black and minority ethnic colleagues. Although I do not hesitate to speak on their behalf if I believe this is the right thing to do, at other times, my silence can allow other (white) colleagues to take responsibility. [Personal communication, April 2009]

Practices

Key organizational practices, with attendant examples, advantages, and disadvantages, are summarized in Tables 1–11.

Table 1.   Ethnically/culturally matched services.

Description	These are services that are based on the assumption of culturally congruent care. Examples include Newham Asian Women's Project, which offers services to South Asian women within East London, or Peace of Mind Somali Mental Health Project at the Tavistock Clinic, which offers services to Somali children, young people, and their families in North London. Staff for these services are drawn from professionals from the same or similar community as the client group, although management of these services are not necessarily also matched.

(continued)

Table 1. (*continued*)

Advantages	Shown to engage and ease the joining process for BME clients (Tamasese & Waldergrave, 1993).
	Shown to improve outcome (Ito & Maramba, 2002).
	Shown to increase client retention rates (Ito & Maramba, 2002).
	Shown to decrease emergency and inpatient services (Ito & Maramba, 2002).
	Provides improvedtraining opportunities for working with culturally diverse groups, as specialist trainings are often provided within house and to outside agencies.
Dilemmas	There is a question around whether black clients may view black workers as part of a white institution and, thus, still regard them with suspicion or mistrust (a process described by Boyd-Franklin, 1989 as "healthy cultural paranoia").
	Black therapists/professionals may feel that they have to make special concessions for clients from their own, or a similar, cultural background, from a sense of guilt about being successful in a white world.
	Internalized racism may contribute to clients not wanting to see a worker from the same background (Thomas, 2002).
	When the client brings extremely sensitive and confidential material to the session, they may prefer to be seen by some body who does not belong to the same community as them. They may feel that they are less likely to be judged or to have their confidences betrayed by somebody who belongs to a different cultural group.
	It is important to consider what place the service has within the wider organization/community of services. Important questions to bear in mind might include: does the service become marginalized? Is it seen as dealing with issues that are not central to the main work of the organization/community? Is the service viewed as holding responsibility for BME issues, thus absolving others from addressing such issues?
	The service may be viewed by others as racist because of positive discrimination.
	Who leads culturally matched services? Should the leaders/directors of such services only be recruited from within the BME community, or is it possible to open up such posts to those from white or white minority groups? It could be argued that a white leader of a team of BME workers replicates a colonizing process. On the other hand, having a white leader could be seen as a way of ensuring that the responsibility is taken on by both white and black workers.

Table 2.   Steering groups attached to ethically/culturally matched services.

Advantages	Engaging a steering group enables a wide range of interested and committed parties to contribute to the shape and the delivery of the service. For example, the Centre for Cross-Cultural Studies at the Institute of Family Therapy drew professionals from a refugee non-government organization (NGO), the National Health Service, and academic institutions. This enabled a range of multi-disciplinary perspectives and the possibility of fostering contacts with other agencies, funding bodies, and universities.
	A steering group that is made up of professionals belonging to other institutions and agencies may highlight the ongoing tension about whether a centre is sufficiently mainstreamed within an organization or whether its role is marginal to the life of the organization.
Dilemmas	When choosing a steering group, it is important to consider the way in which issues of "difference", such as race, culture, gender, or profession may be played out within the group. It is, therefore, essential to think transparently about the group processes both together in the group and also by creating a safe space to think with an outside consultant.

Table 3.   Establishing a "Race" and Culture Steering Group.

Description	This is a sub-group of a staff team that is formed by interested members of the organization to think about issues to do with "race" and culture. The group could meet once every six to eight weeks. The group might flag up issues that are relevant to practice, such as putting up signs in different languages, increasing work with interpreters, thinking about the use of translating services, celebrating world festivals, giving guidance to staff about terminology, keeping up to date with policy/literature, and considering training needs of staff groups. The "Race" and Culture Steering Group might also make presentations to staff teams to enhance their awareness and to disseminate wider thinking about issues of "race" and diversity.
Advantages	The steering group keeps issues of race, culture, and diversity on the organizational agenda.
Dilemmas	Unless the group is set up to regularly elicit feedback from, and incorporate thinking back to, the staff group, there is a danger that responsibility for issues of "race" and diversity becomes lip service, delegated to the group, and is not held by the staff team as a whole.

Table 4.   Culturally matched supervision.

Description	Some organizations provide BME staff with the opportunity to meet with a supervisor from their own cultural background. This is an approach that recognizes that BME staff may need a space with a culturally matched supervisor or consultant to process aspects of their working life.
Advantages	Acknowledges the distinct support needs and experiences of BME staff. McDowell (2004) talks about the need to carve out racially democratic spaces within organizations and identifies that professional support of others from a similar racial background, who may be perceived to have gone through similar experiences, might enable staff to name and process experiences of marginalization or racism. Speaking with a supervisor from a similar ethnic background also provides BME staff with a senior role model.

Table 5.   Cultural consultation.

Description	Some organizations provide all staff with the opportunity to consult with professionals from within or outside the organization when they are stuck with dilemmas that involve issues of "race" and culture either at a clinical or organizational level. The cultural consultants usually have specialist insider knowledge about the cultural group(s) that the staff member is experiencing difficulties with. For example, the former Asian Service at the Tavistock Clinic provided consultation to professionals with regard to working with Bangladeshi clients.
Advantages	Cultural consultation utilizes the expertise of bicultural/bilingual professionals.
Dilemmas	The cultural consultant may not know much about the client group that they are expected to provide cultural consultation about, as they might be from different religious/class backgrounds or subgroups. There is, thus, a danger that the cultural consultant may provide inaccurate or misleading information.

Table 6. Establishing a culturally/racially matched mentor role.

Description	For BME staff working in predominantly white organizations, it could be helpful to assign a mentor who is culturally or racially matched. This is in line with many training institutions that provide a support group for BME trainees to think about their experiences in a formal supportive space. The thinking behind this is threefold: 1. Staff might find that their experiences are marginalized in a white group. 2. It may be helpful to think about the impact of Eurocentric assumptions in the models of work itself, for example, if models are based on individualistic assumptions, does this isolate, or create dilemmas for, people from more collectivist cultures? 3. The role provides senior role models for staff.
Advantages	Acknowledges the distinct support needs and experiences of BME staff. Having a mentor can potentially provide a space for staff to talk about experiences of racism with a senior member of staff whom they may feel is well placed to understand and address the experience of racism. This is in keeping with the observation by MacPherson and his team that problems of institutional racism must be recognized before they can be addressed (MacPherson, 1999).
Dilemmas	Other team members may feel that BME staff is getting preferential treatment and support. This may locate the responsibility on the BME mentor to nurture a culture of understanding and inclusion of BME experiences, rather than it being a shared team responsibility.

Table 7. BME staff group meetings.

Description	These are groups set up for black and BME staff to have a forum where they can meet and share their experiences. These discussions may include experiences of discrimination and racism in the organization, or focus on helpful experiences of inclusion. Meetings could be held as frequently as required, but are usually around once a month. Attendance is voluntary and the leadership of such groups tends to be democratic.
Advantages	Staff group meetings promote the voices of BME staff within an organization. They give BME staff a sense of solidarity and support from those who may have had similar experiences.
Dilemmas	Such a group may be viewed as subversive within an organization and the BME workers could find that they are isolating themselves from the rest of the organization.

Table 8.   Cultural competence training.

Description	As a response to the specific care needs of BME communities, social policy makers have recommended training for mental health professionals in "cultural competence".
Advantages	Staff could learn skills in cultural sensitivity and gain knowledge about specific minority ethnic groups.
Dilemmas	Although the term "cultural competence" is widely used in the current context of training, there is little agreement about what constitutes cultural competence and how it can be taught and evaluated (Bhui, Warfal, Edomyal, McKenzie, & Bhugra, 2007; Gunaratnam, 2008). Training in cultural competence could be yet another "box to tick" with regard to overall training needs. The training may not translate into the complexity of working with those from different BME groups. Training in cultural competence could lead to stereotypic and generalized descriptions of certain BME groups. Those workers who have completed a course in cultural competence may feel that they are now "experts" in the field and that there is no need for co-working, consultation, or supervision when working with BME groups.

Table 9.   Organizing conferences.

Description	Agencies or organizations who would like to promote cross-cultural thinking and awareness within their staff teams may wish to organize a conference on a particular area of interest, for example, "Working with interpreters" or "Meeting the needs of minority ethnic and separated children and adolescents". Conferences could be between one and two days long, and could comprise keynote and plenary speeches and workshops by experts in the field. Speakers from the local, national, and international community are often called upon to speak at such conferences. There is usually an associated charge for participants.
Advantages	Conferences are a relatively easy way to reach out to a large section of the public and to thus promote awareness about intercultural working. Conferences can raise the profile of an institution, or of a culturally matched service within an institution.
Dilemmas	It may require much time and effort to organize a conference. When an organization is not established, or when the roles and responsibilities within a team are blurred, such a task can place additional stress on the team or organization. There may be some professionals/organizations who cannot afford the associated cost of attending such conferences.

Table 10.   Research and publications.

Description	An institution that is mindful of issues of "race" and culture could embark on a piece of research that looks at such issues within a community. For example, the Asian Service at the Tavistock Clinic London, a culturally matched service to meet the needs of the South Asian community, was commissioned by the Department of Education to carry out a piece of research on the reasons for the poor school attendance among the Bangladeshi community.
Advantages	A thorough needs assessment, clinical audit, or service evaluation can translate into providing services or changing existing policy. For example, the research carried out by the Asian Service mentioned above found that students did not attend school on Eid (a major Muslim festival). As a result, the Education Welfare Department recommended compulsory holidays on Eid in schools where there are a high proportion of Muslims.
Dilemmas	Many professionals still find research a daunting prospect and hesitate to design and undertake a piece of research for fear that they do not have the required skills or time. Often time consuming The research question and design have to be carefully constructed in order to be useful.

Table 11.   Reading groups.

Description	An organization could form a reading group or book club to bring together professionals who are interested in reading and discussing books about cultural diversity. For example, there is a reading group attached to the Centre for Cross-Cultural Studies at the Institute of Family Therapy. The group was founded by an anthropologist–psychologist and comprises mental health professionals who come together once a month to read books from the fields of anthropology, sociology, and family therapy. The group will sometimes invite an author of a book that they are currently reading to attend the meeting and engage in a discussion
Advantages	A book club can bring together like minded people engaged in a common task. It is an economical and enjoyable way of raising awareness about issues of cultural diversity. It creates good networking opportunities.
Dilemmas	Should membership of the group be restricted to those within the organization or open to those outside? Should it be a closed or an open group? Should the group Chair be drawn from within or outside the institution?

References

Boyd-Franklin, N. (1989). *Black Families in Therapy: A Multisystems Approach*. New York: Guilford Press.

Bhui, K., Warfal, N., Edomyal, P., McKenzie, K., & Bhugra, D. (2007). Cultural competence in mental health care: a review of model evaluations. *BME Health Services Research, 7*: 15.

Ito, K. L., & Maramba, G. G. (2002). Therapeutic beliefs of Asian American therapists: views from an ethnic-specific clinic. *Transcultural Psychiatry, 39*: 33–73.

Gunaratnam, Y. (2008). From competence to vulnerability: care, ethics and elders from racialised minorities. *Mortality, 13*(1): 24–41.

Fredman, G. (1997). *Death Talk: Conversations with Children and Families*. London: Karnac.

MacPherson, Sir William (1999). *The Stephen Lawrence Inquiry*. London: HMSO.

McDowell, T. (2004). Exploring the racial experience of therapists in training: a critical race theory perspective. *American Journal of Family Therapy, 32*: 305–324.

Tamasese, K., & Waldergrave, C. (1993). Cultural and gender accountability in the "just therapy" approach. *Journal of Feminist Family Therapy, 5*(2): 29–45.

Thomas, L. (2002). Ethnic sameness and difference. In: B. Mason & A. Sawyerr (Eds.), *Exploring the Unsaid: Creativity, Risks and Dilemmas in Working Cross-Culturally* (pp. 49–69). London: Karnac.

Exercises

Most of the exercises included in the manual thus far can be used or adapted by managers and supervisors to use within your teams. Some exercises, such as cultural genograms (p. 33) or Falicov's MECA (p. 51) can be used to enhance your employees' self reflexivity. Others, like the assumptions exercise (p. 49) or the naming exercise (p. 26) can be used within team meetings to bring to the fore the assumptions we bring to working with clients.

You could use papers, books, and films as starting points for team discussions about diversity (see Appendix II for possible resources), or ask a team member to present a piece of work where they were working with a client from a culturally different background as a way to structure the discussion.

We have come up with a few further exercises, outlined below, that could be used by managers and supervisors to help their teams to think about issues of racial cultural diversity.

Exercise 1: Exploring organizational avenues to promote race and culture

Context/organization

This exercise was devised by Sumita Dutta, based on the theoretical ideas in this chapter.

Aim

To help the team to think about which of the above practices (for example, a BME staff group or a reading group) for promoting "race" and culture within an organization is most appropriate for your organizational team/training group to explore.

Instructions

Participants: between 10 and 30; duration: 1–1.5 hours; resources: flipchart paper and pens.

1. Break the team into groups.
2. Depending on how many ideas you want to explore, assign one idea to each group.
3. Ask each group to brainstorm:
    *   their understanding of the service development;
    *   how they think this would promote issues of race and culture within the service/team;
    *   what dilemmas they think might arise.
4. Ask one member of the group to scribe the conversation and be prepared to feed back to the larger group.

Notes for trainers:

*   Thinking about issues of cultural diversity within a team can be an emotive process and may require careful facilitation.
*   It may be useful to invite a consultant to join the manager, or, where this is not possible, for two managers to co-facilitate such a discussion.
*   You may wish to share some of the descriptions offered here with the group before, after or during the exercise.

Exercise 2: Taking positions

Context/organization

This exercise was devised by Reenee Singh, based on David Campbell's (2006) work on positioning in team consultations.

Aim

To explore and to try to resolve differences within teams, with regard to practices around "race" and culture.

Instructions

Participants: 3+; duration: 1–1.5 hours; resources: flipchart and pens.

1. Ask the team to think about a dilemma they are currently experiencing in adopting a positive practice to do with "race" and culture as part of their service development. For example, some members of the team might like to develop an interpreting service, while others may see it as problematic to do so. When the group has come up with one or more dilemmas, write the dilemmas clearly on a sheet of flipchart paper (15 mins).

2. Translate the dilemma(s) into a continuum with two polarities: for example, "Think it is a good idea to use interpreters" as one polarity and "Do not think it is a good idea to use interpreters" as another polarity. Draw a straight, horizontal line on the flipchart, with the polarities written on either end of the line (5 mins).

3. Ask the team to come up, one by one, and mark where they would position themselves on this line. (You may wish to carry out this part of the exercise physically, so that you could ask the group to form a line with those who think it is a good idea to use interpreters on one end, and those who do not, on the other end.) (5–20 mins, depending on the numbers in the team.)

4. Form pairs from within the team/group. The pairs could comprise those from the "most" and "least" ends of the continuum (5 mins).

5. Ask the pairs to interview each other, based on the following questions (15 mins):
   ● How did you arrive at your position?
   ● What would help you to shift your position?

6. Reconvene to the large group and facilitate a team discussion about how the exercise may have changed people's perceptions of the dilemma, and how the group or team now feels in relation to the particular idea for service development (10 mins).

Notes for trainers

- This exercise provides a non-blaming way in which to explore different ideas within the team, with regard to issues of "race" and culture.
- When members of a group or team realize that positions can be shifted, it could prompt them to think about other dilemmas within their team, and ways of resolving their differences.
- It may be useful to invite a consultant to join the manager, or, where this is not possible, for two managers to co-facilitate such a discussion.
- During a long workshop or Away Day, it might be possible to explore a number of different dilemmas.

Reference

Campbell, D. (2006). Locating conflict in team consultations. In: D. Campbell and C. Huffington (Eds.), *Organizations Connected. A Handbook of Systemic Consultation*. London: Karnac.

Exercise 3: Good practice case example

Context/organization

This exercise was devised by Reenee Singh, on the basis of her own experiences of talking about service developments to commissioners and managers.

Aims

- To facilitate a team discussion about possible ways of working with cultural diversity.
- To start a discussion about the fit between different practices and agency contexts.

Instructions

Participants: the entire team; duration: approximately one hour.

1. Invite somebody from another organization, either within your borough or from another borough to come and share an example of how they have worked with cultural diversity in their organizations.
2. Break the team into pairs or groups and discuss:
    (a) How do you think this model might fit with your organization?
    (b) What do you think might be the limitations of transposing such a model into your agency context?

Notes for trainers

- This exercise is relatively easy to facilitate as the focal point for discussion is an example from another organization. The most important

thing to draw out is possible reasons why the case example may or may not fit with your team's organizational context.
- You may want to use more than one case example to facilitate a wider discussion.

Exercise 4: Reflecting on barriers to change.

Context/organization

This exercise was devised by Reenee Singh, based on feedback from participants on courses that she facilitated (see Appendix One).

Aim

To highlight the difficulties in thinking, talking, and working with racial and cultural diversity within teams.

Instructions

Participants: 9–30; duration: approximately 1.5 hours.

1. Ask each member of your team to take five minutes considering the question: "What do you think makes it difficult for us to talk about racial and cultural diversity?"
2. Open up and facilitate a team discussion based on each member's thoughts (20 mins).
3. Break the team into three groups and ask each group to think about what the possible barriers to working with racial and cultural diversity within the organization might be (20 mins).
4. Each group assigns a volunteer to feed back (5 mins).
5. The three volunteers form a circle in the middle of the room and have a reflecting conversation where they discuss the ideas that were thought about in their groups with each other, while the others in the group listen (10–15 mins).
6. The wider group then reflects upon the discussion they have just heard and an open discussion occurs (10–15 mins).

Notes for trainers

- This exercise could provoke strong feelings within the team, as it is about barriers to thinking, talking, and changing.
- It may be useful to invite a consultant to join the manager, or, where this is not possible, for two managers to co-facilitate such a discussion.

Exercise 5: Obstacles and solutions to change

Context/organization

This exercise was adapted by Reenee Singh from an exercise described by Stephen Fitzpatrick. It can be used as an active adjunct to the previous exercise, "Reflecting on barriers to change".

Aims

- To facilitate the team to think about barriers or obstacles to adopting positive practices in working with issues of "race" and culture.
- To help the team to come up with solutions to overcoming the barriers or obstacles to change.

Instructions

Participants: the entire team; total time: approximately 45 mins; resources: sheets of A4 paper and pens.

1. Distribute the A4 sheets and pens to each member of the team (5 mins).
2. In pairs, ask the group to discuss and write down possible obstacles to adopting positive or culturally sensitive practices. Each obstacle should be written down on a separate sheet of A4 paper (5 mins).
3. Ask for volunteers to place their sheets, face up, on the floor, for everybody else in the group to see (10 mins).
4. Now ask the pairs to discuss and write down solutions for each of the obstacles that are on the floor. Each solution should be written on a separate sheet of A 4 paper (5 mins).
5. Ask for volunteers to cover each obstacle, lying on the floor, with a matched solution (10 mins).
6. Facilitate a brief group discussion about the process of the exercise (5 mins).

Note for trainers

This fast paced exercise can bring the barriers and obstacles to life in a few simple steps!

Source and acknowledgement

Sociodrama workshop attended by Stephen Fitzpatrick.

Exercise 6: Team cultural genogram

Context/organization

This exercise was devised by Reenee Singh.

Aims

● To help a team identify the cultural diversity within it.
● To help a team to think about how their own ethnic and cultural backgrounds have an impact on their work with their client group.

Instructions

Participants: 3–15; total time: 1–1.5 hours; resources: flipchart paper and pens.

1. Provide the team with flipcharts and coloured pens (5 mins).
2. Ask each member of the team to choose a colour that they think represents their culture (5 mins).
3. The team should get together and draw a large picture depicting their positions within the organization, in their different colours (30–45 mins, depending on the size of the team and the group process).
4. Group discussion about the process of doing the exercise and how they think the cultural diversity within the team has an impact on their client group (30 mins).

Notes for trainers

● This exercise can provide vivid material for thought!
● The team cultural genogram can be kept and revisited during subsequent team meetings and Away Days.

Exercise 7: Noticing whiteness in organizations

Context/organization

This exercise was devised by Claire Dempster, based on her research and theoretical ideas about whiteness (see p. 11) and adapted by Reenee Singh.

Aims

● To help a team identify the cultural diversity within it.
● To facilitate a team in thinking about how white ethnicities are thought about and recorded.
● To help a team to think about how their own ethnic and cultural backgrounds have an impact on their clinical work.

Instructions

Participants: 6–21; total time: 1–1.5 hours; resources: sheets of paper and pens to write down notes, if necessary.

1. Provide a brief introduction to how thinking about "race", ethnicity, and culture can often miss out on noticing and discussing whiteness, which can still be seen as an invisible norm (5 mins).
2. Split the group into pairs (5 mins).
3. Ask the pairs to consider and discuss the following questions (20 mins).
    - What information does your organization collect about the racial/ethnic mix of staff?
    - How, if at all, is whiteness recorded by your organization, for example, ethnicity codes. How does this compare with other ethnicities?
    - In a team meeting or case discussion, when is the race or ethnicity of the client or practitioner most likely to be referred to and in what context?
    - In a team meeting or case discussion, when is the race or ethnicity of the client and/or practitioner least likely to be referred to?
4. Now reconvene the pairs into the larger group and break them into three groups (5 mins).
5. Ask the groups to think about the effect of noticing whiteness when working with (a) clients—Group 1, (b) colleagues—Group 2 and (c) service managers—Group 3 (10 mins).
6. One volunteer from each group feeds back to the larger group (15 mins).
7. Group discussion (10 mins).

Notes for trainers

- This exercise can be long and complicated, but it is a good exercise to facilitate a group/team in working with people with whom they may not have worked before.
- It can often come as a relief for white people in a team to think that their cultural/ethnic background is being noticed and thought about.
- It is important for the trainer to draw out the implications of noticing whiteness for the team and for clients.

Exercise 8: "Race" and culture timeline

Context/organization

This exercise was devised by Reenee Singh

Aims

- To help teams and managers think about the progress of their work with racial and cultural diversity.
- To help teams and managers plan for the future of their work with racial and cultural diversity.

Instructions

Participants: the entire team (at least six); total time: 45 mins–1 hour; resources: flipchart paper and pens.

1. Break the group into smaller groups of three or four and give each group a piece of flipchart paper and pens (5 mins).
2. Ask each small group to devise and draw a timeline about their agencies thinking and key developments in their practices about racial and ethnic diversity (15 mins).
3. The timeline should consist of dates and activities, for example, 2008—formed reading group/steering group.
4. The timeline should include anticipated future events and plans.
5. A volunteer from each group shares the group's timeline with the larger group (15–20 mins).
6. Group discussion about the history and future with regard to working with racial and cultural diversity (10–15 mins).

Exercise 9: Consultation and competing marginalizations

Context and organization

Developed by Barry Mason as part of the Advanced Training in Supervision at the Institute of Family in London.

Aims

- To help participants take more risks in their work.
- To help participants go beyond simple constructions about oppression and marginalization in order to facilitate a realization that at times we are faced with competing marginalizations in the work that we do.

Instructions

Participants: 3+; total time: approximately half an hour.

1. Break the group into smaller groups of three or four (5 mins).
2. Participants are asked, in small groups, to consider the following scenario and to discuss and explore the potential solutions, dilemmas, and feelings generated by such a scenario (15 mins).

A clinical consultant is working with a team of nine people in the help-ing professions. One of them, a white man, a longstanding member, has a very severe hearing loss. Another (recently arrived) member of the team, a female, is a Muslim, and from choice wears a veil. Unknown to the consultant (although it soon emerges) there has been friction in the team, with the person who has the hearing difficulty unable to understand what his female colleague is saying because he lip reads and cannot see her mouth. A partial solution has been to have the words of the Muslim team member repeated by another colleague. The man with the hearing difficulty is not happy about this because, he says, he now feels marginalized, whereas previously this had not been the case.

If you were the clinical consultant how would you approach this issue?

3. Reconvene the group and ask for feedback from the consultations (10 mins).

Notes for trainers

- This is a powerful exercise that can bring up feelings of discrimination and marginalization within teams.
- It should be used sensitively, especially when there are Muslim members of the team or those with physical disabilities.
- The exercise can be used to highlight the complexities of working with differences within teams.

Reference

Mason, B. (2007). Consultation and competing marginalisations: an exercise. *Context* (Special edition: *Faith, Values and Relationships*), *89*: 38.

Dilemmas in training and pointers for practice

Reenee Singh and Sumita Dutta

Outline

So here it is then—a recipe book for how to train/teach professionals to think about and work with issues of "race" and culture and, indeed, other aspects of diversity. We are hoping that you, the reader/trainer will use this handbook as a guide and resource for designing and delivering trainings to a range of professionals in different contexts. What we have not discussed thus far, and now wish to outline, are some of the dilemmas we regularly encounter while delivering training around diversity. We have clustered these considerations into three main (interrelated) areas: (1) group processes; (2) competing marginalities; (3) structural considerations. We look at each of these areas in turn, drawing from practice dilemmas we ourselves have encountered (identifying details in the practice examples have been anonymized to protect confidentiality). We conclude by presenting twenty main pointers for practice.

Group processes

A trainee once commented,

"Although we learnt a lot about diversity through the course curriculum and through the many exercises that you (the staff team) provided, not once on this course did we talk about what was happening with regard to diversity within the group. The two women from East Europe felt marginalized, partly because of language issues, and the men on our course often dominated group discussions."

The participant's feedback serves as a useful reminder to us about the ways in which groups might need to be empowered to extend their conversations about diversity to include the effects of diversity within the training group itself.

In our experience as trainers of both formal, accredited, family therapy trainings (Years 1 to 4, or Foundation to Advanced) and a myriad of short courses for professionals from many different agency contexts, we have found that issues of diversity within the group will manifest themselves regardless of the duration or formality of the training. Hence, in this postscript, when we speak of diversity within course groups, we could be referring to presentations or courses that range in length from under an hour to four years.

Do these group dynamics emerge anyway, or do they acquire prominence when delivering training on issues of "race" and culture? In our experience, issues of inclusion and exclusion are played out among every group of course participants, and groups will often organize themselves around differences in "race", culture, sexual orientation, religion, class, gender, professional discipline, and so on. However, the differences may become more pronounced during or after a specific training on "race" and culture.

For example, in a recent training, we noticed that the group organized itself in a striking way during a lecture about family diversity. This was an extremely diverse group, with African Caribbean, South American, Asian, Irish, and white English participants. Towards the end of the lecture, in which we explored ways in which the family is constructed differently in different cultures, we noticed that two of the minority ethnic participants were whispering to each other and exchanging hand-written notes. One of the white English participants reproached them for disturbing the rest of the group. After the lecture was over, one of the African Caribbean participants approached us and expressed her view that we should respect and tolerate differences among the group.

With hindsight, we could have "caught" the group process earlier, and addressed it when participants brought it up. We might also have been curious (but not certain) about whether this incident related to the lecture topic itself, and we might have referred back to the original ground rules of the group in which participants actively take ownership of respecting each other's differences and creating a shared space for learning.

In another training, we played an extract from the film *East is East* to illustrate the possible difficulties in intercultural and inter-faith families. A Muslim member of the group described to us becoming acutely aware of being the only Muslim present and expressed the belief that Islam was not represented accurately in the film. The participant felt that the group was replicating the discrimination that Muslims were subjected to within wider society. Here, the material within the film triggered a set of group dynamics based on religious and racial differences. On this occasion, we facilitated a discussion within the group by drawing on ideas around isomorphic processes (Liddle & Saba, 1983). By this, we mean the ways in which relationships can sometimes mirror the content of conversations and replicate similar patterns (such as inclusion or exclusion) or feelings (such as indignation) at different levels. By naming this idea, often used in clinical work, we as a group, including the trainers, had then to consider the levels at which we might be replicating a pattern for this participant in which Islam is singled out for scrutiny in a way that might leave any Muslim in the group feeling uncomfortable.

In other trainings where one person is clearly dominating the "race" talk, we have found it useful to break into pair work, go round each person in the group to get individual feedback, or refer back to the ground rules, where issues of sharing group space will have been negotiated at the beginning. On occasions where one member of the group might take a very authoritative stance on a particular minority position, such as a British minority ethnic member of the group regularly taking up the issues of "race" and culture more than others, we are likely to try to name this process by posing a question such as "We have heard from other BME students that it feels like a terrible burden to always have to bring up issues of "race" and culture; how does this group think we are doing at owning these issues as a course?"

Similarly, there are also times where one person's experience may unwittingly silence another's. For example, a description of one person's experience of racism might make it difficult for others in the group to name their own uncertainties around how to be respectful around issues of "race" and culture. In situations like this where we notice a possible silencing, we are likely to try to name these dynamics tentatively by making comments such as: "In trainings that we have done before, we sometimes notice that people feel afraid of getting things wrong around "race" and culture, particularly when they do not want to offend anyone else's experience of racism." Or "My colleague often describes to me the issues she notices in training around matters of 'race' and culture, where some people, in their attempt to honour other people's experience of racism, often remain silent about their own experiences or struggles."

These attempts to name group dynamics by using the examples of other students, other groups, or colleagues aims to limit any sense of criticism that may be experienced by group members and seeks to give permission for other conversations, or quieter voices in the group, to emerge.

We have also identified and named a somewhat different group dynamic, that is, "denial of racialized difference". In the face of teaching on "race" and culture, course participants will sometimes insist that racial or cultural differences are not important and that they would rather focus on "real" issues, for example, therapeutic engagement, or the child's mental health. In such instances, instead of getting into a polarized position of defending the significance of cultural differences, we find it helpful to adopt a both–and position (Anderson, 1987) where we suggest that it is possible to focus both on cultural differences and on the child's mental health. We point out how inextricably linked the two seemingly disparate ideas may be. We might also reflect on what it means that we, as facilitators, carry the responsibility for naming racial and cultural difference.

Competing marginalities

In the previous section, we have provided some examples from our practice where group dynamics have emerged and made some suggestions about how we might go about addressing these. In this next section, we want to think about a second group of common issues that arise. We call these competing marginalities, and by this we mean when marginalities within the group not only emerge, but also go head to head in competition with each other.

For example, sometimes, a group member may feel that they want to share in detail a personal or professional experience of discrimination, which might be very emotive. We have noticed that this can sometimes lead to competition among group members to describe equally or more difficult experiences as a way of staying in the conversation. When this type of competitiveness emerges, we have found it useful to think about a continuum, or range, of experiences which can fall somewhere between explicit and subtle forms of discrimination (Figure 4). We might notice, or ask the group to notice, where most of their descriptions so far seem to be falling. The hope is that this reflection and active scaling on a continuum can enable people to notice any patterns that might be emerging and make space for "lesser" experiences to be voiced.

Explicit/subtle

Another common theme that we encounter with competing marginalities is when racial and cultural descriptions of discrimination are felt to dominate over other forms of discrimination, such as sexism or homophobia. For example, conversations may emerge around the relative acceptability of a sexist or homophobic comment in public arenas in comparison to, say, a racist or anti-religious comment. We have found that making space for these comments to be processed among the group serves to lift the conversation to another level of context, which we would term societal, and often enables participants to express anger and make valuable critiques of social values and norms. We have also found that participants, such as a BME female, may reflect upon the intersections of discrimination she has experienced as *both* a British Ethnic Minority *and* a female, thus serving to illustrate the concept of multiplexity (Akamatsu, 1998) in which various marginalities, not just "race" and culture, intersect in people's lives.

Explicit  Subtle

Figure 4.   Explicit/subtle.

In other situations we have noticed that sometimes the competitiveness may be directed toward us, as course facilitators. In a hypothetical hierarchy of experienced discrimination, we have found that the participants' perceptions of us as middle class South Asian professional women might mean that, for some participants, our experiences of racism and discrimination cannot compare to their own. Other Asian participants may see us as part of a "white" world, and, hence, implicated in a form of internal racism. On the other hand, the white participants in the group may position themselves alongside us, or, if they feel in a minority position within a predominantly black and minority ethnic group, may feel rejected and misunderstood by us as the course leaders.

A variation on the theme of competing marginalization is a process that we would describe as perceptions of positive discrimination. In our experience, the participants on a course may feel that a particular black or minority ethnic student receives preferential treatment on the basis of her racial and ethnic background. There is a sense, among the course participants, that it is unfair for that participant to "play the race card" in order to be granted concessions or privileges. As course leaders, this dilemma places us in a delicate position of having to balance the real or perceived injustice and discrimination towards one student with the needs of the whole group. There are no easy answers to how to work with these types of alliances and beliefs. However, we have become more proactive in our approach over the years, and try to acknowledge early on in the life of a training group the ways in which our own cultural frameworks will colour how we hear what each other has to say. We might carry out an assumptions exercise (see p. 49) in which participants can safely name assumptions that clients might make on first sight about us as professionals. This type of exercise enables cultural assumptions to be named early in the life of a training group (via a safe distance) and, most importantly, seeks to model an idea that all of us will be speaking and owning the things that we say from a limited, non-expert, position as an individual. This is a particularly important precedent to refer back to if competing truths about cultural experience begin to emerge in the group.

We have also found it helpful to talk on an individual basis to course participants who seem to find it difficult to relate to us in a group setting. This is a useful tool, as we have found that it often uncovers broader struggles that the participant is having in relation to wider experiences of discrimination. These conversations allow a space in which these experiences can be heard respectfully, and creates possibilities for the participant to try out different responses within the group discussed. Alternatively, further support for the participant can be sought through the appropriate channels.

Structural considerations

Having looked at group dynamics and competing marginalities, we now review some of the structural considerations that we bear in mind when organizing and delivering training courses around diversity. We have used sub-headings in this section to denote the key areas we are trying to highlight.

Diverse groups: forming and naming diversity

We realize that it is not always possible to choose the group makeup, but, in our experience, the more diverse and heterogeneous the group, the more likely it is that participants will have the opportunity to bump up against differences with each other and, hence, address them. If possible, try to mix up participants within the whole group, small group, and pair exercises. If there is a fixed sub-group, such as a tutor group, then careful consideration should be given to the diversity and cultural mix of these groups.

It is also important to define difference within the group at an early stage of the group's formation. Exercises such as "Being British" (see p. 48), or discussions about whiteness (see pp. 37–38), are helpful in naming differences in a playful way and can also enable "hidden minorities" to emerge. For example, there may be participants from different European countries who, although they are white, may feel less privileged than those who are English and grew up in the UK. There may also be people for whom naming their sexual orientation, class, disability, and so on are an important initiation into the group.

Diverse groups: naming the barriers

In some training courses, especially advanced professional trainings, access for some BME students may be more difficult than for

their white counterparts. This may have to do with entry require-
ments and processes, or even with the reputation that certain training courses develop. Similarly, assessment procedures may be
stacked against those students from minority ethnic or disadvan-
taged backgrounds, or those whose first language is not English.

Indeed, it is important for professionals to consider their own
diversity as a staff group. We believe that having a diverse staff
group models to students the possibilities of dialogues across
difference. Although many of us may be delivering training inde-
pendently, we can still model to students the way in which we think
about the diversity of the organization from which we come. For
example, when we describe our work contexts, we are always careful to name the cultural and ethnic populations we serve and
present diverse and relevant case material, where appropriate

Course content

We cannot emphasize enough the importance, when designing a
course on "race" and culture, or other aspects of diversity, to leave
plenty of time for the participants to be able to reflect on how the
content of the lecture/workshop resonates with their own professional and personal experiences. Although discussions can arise
that need careful facilitation, sometimes, as trainers, we may hesi-
tate to allow enough time and space for fear of opening up something that cannot be contained. The trainees, in turn, respond to our
fears, so that little that is meaningful can be talked about.

Although it is our responsibility as trainers to raise and address
difficult issues in an honest and sensitive way, it is also up to the
trainees to respond to these discussions. We have to be aware of our
positions and the limitations of our role in a training context. At the
outset of any training, we need to make it clear to the participants
that their roles as students/trainees come with the expectations of
tolerance and respect towards each other's deeply held and cher-
ished beliefs.

Further to the above, it is also important to scrutinize the content
of the course to ensure that diversity issues are integrated seam-
lessly. We feel that it is important to ensure that there are racial and
cultural critiques of every topic, so that issues of "race" and culture
are integrated at every level, rather than treated as token add-ons.

Supporting students

One of the ways that we have found to support the BME students is to set up and provide an ongoing student group for BME members. This can work very well in providing students/ trainees with a space where they can process the complexity of being different with like-minded trainees/students, both within the course they are studying and across courses within the institution. It is important for this group to be as inclusive as possible, and not divided solely along the lines of colour. Thus, it really is for anybody who considers themselves to be from a "minority ethnic group". This raises the issue of self definition. It is not up to us, as trainers, to prescribe whether students belong in this group, but this should be a fluid process of students feeling that they can speak and be heard within a supportive group. One such group, for all students/trainees who define themselves as black or minority ethnic and who are enrolled on any course within the Tavistock, is facilitated by Britt Krause at the Tavistock Centre.

We have also found it useful to have a list of wider therapeutic, advocacy, and support groups available to trainees as part of their course materials. We usually put this under a section entitled "Further reading and resources". The aim of this is to provide trainees with access to support without them having to name their need for further assistance in a public manner.

Supporting trainers

There are times when we get stuck as trainers and we feel that it is helpful to know that we have a space to talk to peers about doubts and dilemmas. These spaces can be in supervision and/or through peer consultation. We have found that these are particularly useful spaces to access when one has to manage complex group dynamics, including competitiveness or aggressiveness against the trainer. Issues of power, hierarchy, and competition can also arise among the staff group teaching on issues of diversity, and be played out in ways that mirror the diversity (or lack of it) within the team. Peer consultation is extremely useful in such cases, as it is when one is setting up a course, and can help to provide another perspective on issues regarding diversity.

On a wider level, it is important to consider training opportunities and spaces where we can come together as trainers and learn from each other about working with diversity in training contexts. Given the current dearth of such platforms, we plan to set up a training weblog in order to exchange ideas about what has worked in our different contexts, and to meet occasionally to discuss these difficult issues in greater depth.

Pointers for practice

1. Create spaces to talk about the effects of diversity from the beginning of the training.
2. Remember that if you are teaching a group, group dynamics will emerge even if your course is minutes long. Group process may form around the ideas that you present.
3. Keep an eye on issues of inclusion and exclusion amongst group participants; this can involve ways in which participants exclude themselves or are excluded.
4. Catch group processes early and address them as they arise.
5. Set ground rules in which all group members, alongside the trainer, take responsibility for sharing group space and naming group processes.
6. Look out for isomorphic group processes; that is, notice and name the times in which interpersonal or group relationships might also be mirroring wider social patterns of inclusion and exclusion.
7. Remember that pair work and individual feedback are good tools to stop group dynamics from becoming entrenched.
8. Attempt to name difficult group processes by using the example of others: for example, other groups, other students, or other colleagues.
9. Avoid taking an "either/or" position with regard to racial and cultural issues in a group discussion, and aim instead for a "both–and" position.
10. Introduce the idea of continuums of experience so that people can notice if they are becoming organized by one extreme.
11. Work with the idea of multiplexity; that is, the intersection of different levels of diversity in the participants' lives.

12. As a trainer, be transparent about your own background (including gender, culture, class, and sexual orientation) and be open to the idea of how this might have an impact on how the participants hear what you have to say.

13. Select diversity within your training group, so that there is a range of experiences for participants to draw on and the opportunities to learn from each other.

14. Give participants the opportunity to define their own cultural differences and similarities fairly early on within a training course, while emphasizing that these similarities and differences can shift and evolve over the training period.

15. Embrace diversity within your staff group.

16. Present case material of your own work with diverse populations and facilitate the links that the participants make between the case material and their own lives.

17. Do allow enough space and time to process personal and professional connections to issues of diversity.

18. Think about what possible spaces your organization offers students from marginalized backgrounds.

19. Keep in mind the limitations of your role and allow the participants to take some of the responsibility for their own learning.

20. Do not problem solve on your own. Draw on the experience of your peers and supervisors for other perspectives and for consultation.

References

Akamatsu, M. N. (1998). The talking oppression blues: including the experience of power/powerlessness in the teaching of "cultural sensitivity". In: M. McGoldrick (Ed.), *Re-Visioning Family Therapy. Race, Culture and Gender in Clinical Practice* (pp. 414–431). London: Guilford Press.

Anderson, T. (1987). The reflecting team: dialogue and meta dialogue in clinical work. *Family Process*, 26: 415–428.

Liddle, H. A., & Saba, G. S. (1983). On context replication: the isomorphic relationship of training and therapy. *Journal of Strategic and Systemic Therapies*, 2: 3–11.

Training courses taught by Reenee Singh and Sumita Dutta at the Centre for Cross-Cultural Studies at IFT

Therapeutic Skills for Working with Refugee Families: London, September–December 2003.

Therapeutic Skills for Working with Refugee Families: Cardiff, December 2003–March 2004.

Therapeutic Skills for Working with Refugee Families: London, January to April 2004.

Therapeutic Skills for Working with Refugee Families: Manchester, July–December 2004.

Therapeutic Skills for Working with Refugee Families: London, September–December 2004.

Working with South Asian Children and Families: November 2006 and February 2008, Tavistock Clinic.

Therapeutic and Cross-Cultural Skills for Working with Refugee Families: Course for Refugee Council, April–July 2007.

"Race" and Culture. One day of a Foundation level Agency based training in Systemic Psychotherapy for RELATE counsellors: August 2007.

The Issues of Language and Interpretation. Lecture for MSc. Students at the Institute of Family Therapy: September 2007.

Gender, Power and Culture: Lecture for Intermediate Family Therapy students, Institute of Family Therapy: November 2007.

Working in a Multicultural Society: Implications for Systemic Practice. Conference organised by the Centre for Cross-Cultural Studies on 2 November 2007.

The Dilemmas of Multicultural Living: Workshop for RELATE counsellors: November 2007.

Coupleness in the 21st Century: Conference for University of Leeds: January 2008.

London Borough of Merton: Issues of "race" and culture for social workers, February 2008.

Working with Minority Ethnic Children and Families: City University, March 2008.

Television, film and book resources

In addition to the films and books mentioned in the text, here are some additional resources:

ABCD (1999). Directed by Krutin Patel. This is the story of an Indian family living in the suburbs of New Jersey.

All My Loved Ones (Vsichni moji blízci) (Czech Republic/Slovakia/ Poland, 1999). Directed by Matej Minac. True story of Nicholas Winton, who saved hundreds of Czech Jewish children from the Nazis.

American Adobo (2001). Director, Laurice Guillen. A story of five Filipino American friends searching for identity.

Amistad (1998). Directed by Steven Spielberg. Chronicles the 1839 revolt on board a slave ship bound for America.

Anita & Me (2002). Directed by Metin Huseyin. Based on the novel by Meera Syal Explore the world of twelve-year-old Meena, who has moved to England with her Indian family.

Avalon (1990). Directed by Barry Levinson. The story of several generations of a Jewish family.

Barriers (1998). Directed by Alan Baxter. A racial drama set among youths in New York.

Bend It Like Beckham (2002). Story of a teenage Indian girl growing up in Britain.

Bhaji on the Beach (1995). Directed by Gurinder Chadha. A comedy about a group of Indian women, living in England, who are brought together by a day at the beach.

Black & White (1991). Written and directed by Boris Frumin. The relationship between a young Soviet émigré and an African-American building superintendent.

Brothers in Trouble (1996). Directed by Udayan Prasad. Paints a vivid portrait of the secret lives and loves of a group of illegal Pakistani immigrants in 1960s' Britain.

Centre for Cross Cultural Studies, IFT weblog. Includes information about training events and the book club.

Chutney Popcorn (1999). Directed by Nisha Ganatra. A comedy about the cultural struggles between immigrant parents and their Americanized children and the strength of family ties.

Context, 44 (1999). *Sowing the Seeds of Cultural Competence.* Association of Family Therapy publication. This issue includes a wonderful list of resources.

Crash (2004), Directed by Paul Haggis. A car accident brings together a group of strangers in Los Angeles in this look at racial tolerance in contemporary America.

Crossing Delancy (1988). Directed by Joan Micklin Silver. The Jewish grandmother of a thirty-something-year-old woman in New York decides her granddaughter should be married, and hires a matchmaker.

Downfall (Untergang) (Germany / Italy / Austria, 2004). Directed by Oliver Hirschbiegel. Set in Hitler's bunker in 1945, during the brutal and harrowing last days of the Third Reich as seen through the eyes of Hitler's secretary, Traudl Junge.

Driving Miss Daisy (1989). Directed by Bruce Beresford. Set in Atlanta in the 1950s, a story about a relationship between a Jewish woman and her African-American driver.

East is East (1999). Directed by Damien O'Donnell. Story of a Pakistani family growing up in England.

Eat Drink Man Woman (2002). Directed by Ang Lee. Tale following the life and loves of a Taiwanese family in America.

Earth (1998). Directed by Deepa Metha. Story following the lives of several families in Lahore from 1947 onwards.

Educational Failure and Working Class White Children in Britain (2006). A deeply insightful and entertaining account of white working class life in Bermondsey, London, written by the anthropologist, Gillian Evans. Published by Palgrave Macmillan.

Far From Heaven (2002). Directed by Todd Haynes. Cathy is the perfect 1950s housewife who has a friendship with her African-American gardener.

Fire (1996). Directed by Deepa Metha. Passionate story set in India following the liveS of two women drawn together.

Fish Bowl (2005). Directed by Kayo Hatta. Story of an eleven-year-old girl growing up in Hawaii.

Freedom Song (2000). Directed by Phil Alden Robinson. A dramatization of American small-town citizens during the civil rights struggle in the early 1960s.

Freedom Writers (2007). Director, Richard LaGravenese. Dramatization of a true story about a teacher in a racially divided school.

Gandhi (1982). Directed by Richard Attenborough. This film follows Gandhi's life from young lawyer through his historic struggle to free India from colonial rule.

Goodness Gracious Me (BBC Television, 1998–2000). Produced by Anil Gupta; directed by Nick Wood. A British television comedy series presenting a satirical exploration of racial stereotypes in Britain, as seen from an Indian point of view.

In the Heat of the Night (1967). Directed by Norman Jewinson. An African-American detective is asked to investigate a murder in a racist southern town.

I Is For India (2007). Directed by Sandhya Suri. Wonderful home movie footage revealing aspects of immigration in England in the 1970s and onwards.

Interpreter of Maladies (2000). Pulitzer Prize winning collection of short stories following the lives of Indian-Americans.

Little Jerusalem (La Petite Jerusalem) (France, 2005). Directed by Karin Albou. In a Paris suburb nicknamed Little Jerusalem, a family of Sephardic Orthodox immigrants shares a low-income apartment.

Lost Embrace (El abrazo partido) (Argentina/France/Italy/Spain, 2004). Directed by Daniel Burman. Ariel is a young man who lives in a Jewish working-class section of Buenos Aires.

Love + Hate (UK/Ireland, 2005). Directed by Dominic Savage. Looks at race relations in working-class northwest England as seen through the stories of seventeen-year-old Naseema, a second generation British-Pakistani Muslim.

Mendy (Mendeleh) (2003). Directed by Adam Vardy. The story of a young Brooklyn Hasid, as he struggles to adapt and find his place in modern secular society.

Mississippi Burning (1988). Directed by Alan Parker. The dramatization of the case of the murder of three young civil rights workers.

Mississippi Masala (1991). Directed by Mira Nair. An interracial love story; an African American businessman falls for a beautiful Indian immigrant.

Mistress of Spices (USA/UK, 2005). Directed by Paul Mayeda Berges. Tilo is an immigrant from India, and a shopkeeper, who is also the "Mistress of Spices". The spices, which she gives to her customers, help them to satisfy their needs and desires. But then her life changes when she "breaks all the rules" by falling in love with Doug, an American man. Based on the novel by Chitra Banerjee Divakaruni.

Monsoon Wedding (2002). Directed by Mira Nair. Love, lust, and hope envelop an upper middle-class Indian family.

My Beautiful Laundrette (1986). Directed by Stephen Frears, screenplay by Hanif Kureishi. The story of an immigrant family in the UK.

My Own Country (1998). Directed by Mira Nair. A small-town doctor, making the adjustment of coming from India to the rural town of Johnson City, Tennessee.

My Son the Fanatic (1999). Directed by Udayan Prasad. Story of a Pakistani cab driver's struggle to find meaning in the UK.

Rabbit Proof Fence (2002). Australia's government policy regarding mixed race Aboriginal children. |

Persepolis (2007). An animated film based on Marjane Satrapi's autobiographical graphic novel. The story is set against the backdrop of the Iranian Revolution.

Sammy and Rosie Get Laid (1987). Directed by Stephen Frears. A cultural look at London in the 1980s.

Self Made Man. My Year Disguised as a Man (2006). A fascinating account of a woman's experiment in disguising herself as a man. London: Atlantic Books.

Sunshine (Germany/Austria/Canada/Hungary, 2000). Directed by István Szabó. Compelling epic about generations of a Hungarian Jewish family caught up in the upheavals and false hopes of the war-swept twentieth century.

The Buddha of Suburbia (UK, TV, 1993). Directed by Roger Michell. Based on the novel by Hanif Kureishi, the story of a South Asian British family.

The Color Purple (1985). Directed by Steven Spielberg. Story of two sisters living in the rural South of America. Based on the novel by Alice Walker.

The Counterfeiters (Die Fälscher) (Austria/Germany, 2007). Director, Stefan Ruzowitzky. *The Counterfeiters* is the true story of the largest counterfeiting operation in history, set up by the Nazis in 1936.

The Hurricane (1999). Directed by Norman Jewison. The true story of Rubin "Hurricane" Carter, an African-American boxer, who was wrongfully convicted of murder.

The Kumars at No. 42 (BBC Television, 2001). Written by Richard Pinto, Sharat Sardana, Sanjeev Bhaskar; directed by Lissa Evans. In this British television sit-com, the Kumars, a fictional immigrant family, have bulldozed their back garden to build a studio for their spoilt son Sanjeev, who fancies himself a celebrity chat show host.

The Man Who Cried (UK/France, 2000). Directed by Sally Potter. A Russian Jewish father immigrates to America in 1923, with a promise to send for his mother and young daughter when he is settled.

The Namesake (India / USA, 2006). Directed by Mira Nair. The tale of a second generation Indian-American.

The Pianist (France/Germany/UK/Poland, 2002). Directed by Roman Polanski. Story of a Polish Jew.

Water (2005). Directed by Deepa Metha. The film examines the plight of a group of widows forced into poverty at a temple in the holy city of Varanasi, India.

Guide to drawing a basic family genogram

Rules:

- Women and girls are circles, Men and boys are squares. Ages can be placed inside the squares and circles. Important information should be written below the box/circle, for example, illness, occupation.
- Marriage is marked by a straight line between two individuals.

- Separation is marked between couples with a single line. Divorce is marked between couples with a double line. Dates can be added if preferred.

- Children are marked with a line coming down from the parental union, the eldest on the left hand side of the sibling group. This means the eldest generation are at the top of the page and the youngest at the bottom. For example:

Grandparents

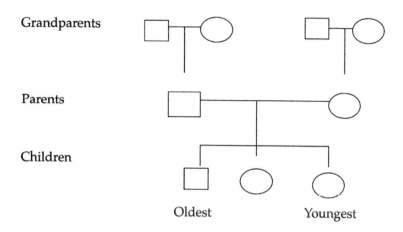

Parents

Children

Oldest   Youngest

- Death can be marked by a cross or RIP. You may also wish to mark the cause of death, for example, cancer, civil war, accident.

- Country or place of residence including transitions can be marked by an arrow downwards, with a date if preferred.
- Relationship patterns should also be marked.

The Social GRRAACCEESS

Gender
Race
Religion
Age
Ability
Class
Culture
Ethnicity
Education
Sexuality
Spirituality

This acronym, and its variations, has been developed between Burnham (1992, 1993) and Roper-Hall (1998, 2008) since its origins in 1990. The above is Burnham's version of the acronym.